D1453141

Checkmate in Prague

Checkmate in Prague

▪▫▪▫▪▫▪▫▪▫▪▫▪▫▪▫▪▫▪▫▪▫▪▫

THE MEMOIRS OF A GRANDMASTER

Luděk Pachman

Translated by
Rosemary Brown

MACMILLAN PUBLISHING CO., INC.
New York

Macmillan Publishing Co., Inc.
866 Third Avenue, New York, N.Y. 10022

Library of Congress Cataloging in Publication Data
Pachman, Luděk
  Checkmate in Prague
  Translation of Jetzt kann ich sprechen.
  1. Pachman, Luděk. 2. Chess. 3. Czechoslovak
Republic—Politics and government—1945-
I. Title.
GV1439.P32A3513 1975   794.1'092'4 (B)   75-23432
ISBN 0-02-594300-6

First American Edition 1975

Printed in the United States of America

Contents

■■■■■■■■■■■■■■■■■■■■■■■■■■■■■■■■■

1. A Chess Player in the Making

At an international tournament a journalist once asked me how I came to play chess. I told him that my aunt had taught me, but that hers was a somewhat different game—she put bishops in the place of knights and vice versa. The Estonian grandmaster Paul Keres, who heard the conversation, remarked with his typical dry humour: 'Of course, one needs to bear that in mind when reading your books on chess.'

Aunt Sláva had the reputation in our family for being something of a terror. For one thing, she smoked, which was still not usual among women in our country, while rumour also had it that she was a Red and to blame for the Russian Revolution. That was because she had lived in Odessa, but, being a member of the Left Social Revolutionaries, she was sent packing by the Bolsheviks when they turned on their former allies. Back home, after a stop for delousing, she joined Grandad in Mladá Boleslav.

When I was five or six, she really did teach me chess. My other adversary was Dad, whose favourite remark was: 'That looks bad; it's high time I sacrificed something.'

My brother deigned only occasionally to play with me, and I used to get very cross. The trouble was that he would always attack with two or three pawns and I had no idea how to reply. I protested and demanded a ban on these pawn attacks, but he refused to accept a new rule of that kind. Once it boiled up into a terrible quarrel. I repaid a cuff on the ear by a blow in the stomach and then saved myself by jumping out of the window right into a bed of roses.

At grammar school I had two adversaries. One was the maths master, who enjoyed playing with us after school, and in June, when examinations were over, during lessons. He was inclined to take his defeats to heart. But the best player in the class was the son of our divinity teacher. He usually beat me. I always played the Danish Gambit, sacrificing two pawns, but as a rule got no compensating attack.

It was only when I had transferred to technical school that I really got stuck into the game. I borrowed books, played over a hundred games from various magazines, and then I joined a club. For one season I played in the chess club Charousek in Mladá Boleslav, and at the beginning of 1940 I was recruited to the village club Duras Čistá. It was unique in its way; the village of Čistá had no more than 900 inhabitants and 110 of them belonged to the chess club.

At the time I was living in Mladá Boleslav, but I used to go home to my birthplace, Bělá pod Bezdězem, on Saturday afternoons, and every Sunday morning at 7.30 I would set out to cover the fifteen miles to Čistá. We cycled to matches with other north Bohemian clubs; on these occasions our landlord at home obliged by lending me a bike. First I played on second board after the champion, Grolmus, but then I won the club championship and challenged him to a match. Evidently as a result of my intensive studies, things were beginning to go excellently with me, so Grolmus lost one game after another.

The technical school was a real hotbed of chess. Mr. Soukup, our teacher, was a former chessmaster of Mladá Boleslav. He always stood up for me when a master hostile to the game caught me playing during lessons. To lend some interest to these encounters, I had to teach my friend Jirka to play. When our class teacher separated us, I used to play blindfolded, calling out the moves to Jirka who kept the set in the back row.

In the spring of 1941 we had a north Bohemian cup tournament, which I managed to win. Then three more wins at matches in our region marked my first real success. I resolved to train even harder. While my friends went out with the girls or to the local wine cellar, I sat at home studying, making notes, analysing my own and other people's games. Membership of one club was no longer enough for me; I belonged to Duras, but visited Charousek too. In the autumn of 1941 I won a championship there against strong competition, then in 1942 came the championship of Mladá Boleslav. But that was not really a true victory. Things had not gone well for me in the preliminary group; the last game was adjourned, I had one pawn less and could hope only for a draw, while I needed a full point to take me on to the next round. I arrived for the finish depressed and resigned to failure. But suddenly, a miracle—my opponent, Hladík, started playing very quickly, he made a mistake in a quite simple position, then a second, a third, after which he resigned. That gave me such a boost that I conceded only one drawn game in the final round. Later, I learnt that there had been no miracle. The committee men had wanted me in the final, so Hladík had sacrificed himself—it made no difference to him. In due course I discovered that agreed results are not much rarer in chess than in, for instance, professional boxing.

In the autumn of 1942, I won the north Bohemian championship in a tough fight. By that time I was also composing exercises and studies which I sent to *Šach* (*Chess*) and other papers. But there were some problems connected with my chess life—the worst being that I was hard put to it to pay even the most modest expenses at the club. I saved on the bus fare by walking, but when my one pair of shoes had to be mended, I was forced to stay away from school for the day with the excuse of illness.

Over Christmas 1942 a tournament was held in Prague at which the great Alekhine and the nineteen-year-old German, Klaus Junge, fought for first place. I was able to go and watch thanks to the prize money from the north Bohemian championship. I liked the look of Klaus—what if I were to ask for his autograph, or inquire about that variant in the Nimzo-Indian? But no—he was German. Alekhine, being a Slav, was one of us. I had no knowledge at the time that he had written articles accusing Jews of cheating at chess. Not daring to speak to the great man, I managed at least to get near him.

Alekhine and Klaus met in the last round—everything depended on this game. Junge had a whole point advantage, so the world champion had to win. It was one of his great games. First he sacrificed a pawn, then rook for minor piece, and suddenly, he had a forced mate in seven moves. In a great state of excitement, I started to tell people at the top of my voice which moves would lead to mate. The tournament director rushed up to throw me out, but some of the spectators persuaded him to let me stay. That night I lay awake with all sorts of combinations buzzing in my head; what worried me most was the thought of whether I would ever be able to play against an Alekhine or a Junge.

In April 1943 another championship tournament was due to be held in Prague, at which Alekhine—holder of the world title since 1927—and his official challenger of the immediate pre-war period, Paul Keres, were expected. My club was informed that parallel with the big event there would be another to give promising young players a chance to play some of the masters. The club entered my name and, with the help of chess enthusiasts among our teachers, arranged for me to be given leave from school. I was due to take the school-leaving examination in two months, but ultimately the headmaster gave his permission, adding strict instructions that, when not playing chess, I must study hard throughout the three weeks.

On arrival in Prague, I went with Karel Opočenský, a leading player with whom I had made friends when he visited north Bohemia, to seek accommodation. To my dismay, I learnt that the subsidiary tournament had been cancelled because some of the stronger players had not been able to get leave from work. That knocked me out completely—I had been looking forward so much not only to playing with real masters, but also to watching Alekhine, Keres, Foltys, Opočenský and the others.

Observing my distress, Opočenský remarked that someone had just dropped out of the championship tournament; he would call the director, Kende, to suggest he might take me instead.

Kende was the official who had wanted to chuck me out in December. It seemed impossible that such a severe gentleman would help me. But Opo (that was his nickname), lifted the receiver and introduced me as follows: 'Of course, Pachman won't make many points, probably he'll end up in last place, but he's young and that'll be an attraction.'

Mr. Kende wanted to see me before deciding. He was a tall, lean gentleman, very talkative. Having looked me over, asked about my chess experience and my ideas about the game, he said: 'Well, I'll give you a try, but you mustn't disgrace us.'

He added that I would stay at the Palace Hotel, for food and pocket money I would get 2,000 crowns—the amount stunned me—but I couldn't appear in the clothes I was wearing.

Again I was cast into despair. The suit I had on was not only my best, it was my one and only, because the other had given up the ghost a month previously. Mr. Kende asked if I had any relatives who might help. Yes—Uncle Miroslav lived in Prague! He lent me his son's suit, which made me feel like a real man of the world.

Then the tournament swallowed me up—I realized that this was another world, isolated and closed in upon itself.

In the first round I met chessmaster Průcha—not a top-ranker, I had not heard his name before. Was this my chance, right at the outset? I launched a bold attack, four pawns on the king's wing marched forward more or less in the style brother Vladimír had used to wipe the board with me in the old days. Průcha made seemingly timid moves, then, with a sudden sacrifice of rook for minor piece on the opposite wing, he soon had my position in ruins. Pondering this misfortune, it dawned on me that I could not play here as I had in our local clubs. Would I ever be a match for these people?

The sensation in the first round was the success of the young Moravian master, Jiří Fichtl, who was only three years older than myself. He played black against Alekhine, defended himself from all attacks and accepted the proffered draw in a position where he still had a slight advantage. In the second round I was to meet this talent, and with the handicap of playing black.

This time it was my opponent who was determined to settle matters quickly. His tactics were almost a repetition of my own on the previous day. Against the same opening, the Sicilian Defence, he advanced pawns, but only three, leaving the fourth in reserve. Though hard pressed, I resolved to fight back. I found a seemingly rather odd, but actually promising, knight's manoeuvre from one wing to the corner field on the opposite side of the board. Then came a breakthrough on the queen's wing and —as luck would have it—sacrifice of rook for minor piece, after which I was in control and won the game.

The spectators were taken aback—having drawn with Alekhine, Fichtl had lost to this outsider! Someone came up to me, saying: 'Very good. Don't give in; you'll play better than all of them one day.' Then he introduced himself—he was Amos Pokorný, a chessmaster of the older generation.

Having won another three games, I drew the sixth, then, in the seventh round, I played black with the then master of the Protectorate of Bohemia and Moravia, Opočenský. Playing an opening almost unknown to me, he stood in a better position, but a tactical oversight lost him a piece, and soon he resigned. Half in earnest, he told me off—how dare I, a mere whipper-snapper, deprive him of his high placing.

'If you don't win against Foltys, you'd better keep out of my way,' he concluded.

Foltys was Opo's great rival who, at a tournament in Poděbrady, had been third among the grandmasters after Alekhine and Flohr. To beat him was out of the question. When we met a few days later, I managed, by dint of intense concentration, to play my best game to date. It even appeared later in a textbook on strategy.

After this, the great Alekhine invited me to his room. He got me to demonstrate my game, made a few comments, praised me, and then showed me his game, explaining several hidden combinations and also accepting praise. Mrs. Alekhine was there with her two cats. I had to hold one for a bit and the wretch scratched me, but it was a marvellous evening, something in the nature of a high-point in my life so far.

Alekhine took to inviting me in every day. We always analysed something and I soon discovered that it was no good disagreeing with him because it made him angry. So I just listened reverently to what he said. He invited me for coffee, too. In the Luxor café, it seemed, one could get real coffee under the counter—an expensive luxury for which I had to foot the bill. Alekhine, I discovered, made a point of not paying. Usually there was someone with him, otherwise he simply walked out of the restaurant. The waiters knew him, so they sent the bill to the tournament director. I learnt also from a very annoyed Mr. Kende that by threatening to walk out of the tournament, Alekhine had extracted a 5,000 crown addition to his original 40,000 crown fee. Luckily I was saved by an unexpected patron. He was Mr. Stork, a trader and landowner, who presented me with an enormous salami in recognition of my achievement, plus an invitation to lunch every day at his house. The meals were better than any I have eaten even in peacetime, and by doing without supper I was able to pay for Alekhine's coffee.

I made the acquaintance of several other chess personalities. Once, at six in the morning, someone hammered on my door. I opened to find the German master, Fritz Sämisch, outside.

'Go at once to the post office and send a telegram home,' came the command.

Only half awake, I wondered why a telegram.

'Telegraph as follows: "Send cigarettes immediately." '

'But sir, I don't smoke!' Of course, he brushed aside my objection at once by saying he did smoke and he had run out of cigarettes.

Everyone knew that Sämisch was a chain-smoker. When meditating over difficult situations, he would let ash fall on his trousers and on the board, then, absent-mindedly, he would blow it at his opponent and continue with his thinking. He was always pressed for time. Two and a half hours for forty-five moves, which was the custom then (now the pace is usually slower, only forty moves) was never enough for him. He lost one game in Prague by exceeding the time limit after twenty moves, and another at the thirteenth move, which must be a world record. Once I saw him ponder for a full hour over a quite familiar position at his fourth move. When I asked him about it afterwards, he said:

'You know, I happened to think of one of Bogolyubov's games where he sacrificed a piece at the twenty-third move. It struck me that the sacrifice wasn't right, so I considered all the possibilities.'

15

On my wondering what a sacrifice at the twenty-third move had to do with considering a fourth move, he told me that he always thought about whatever interested him at the moment.

Shortly after that early morning call, Sämisch came to sit by me in the Luxor. I was none too pleased, because in those days I was not particularly anxious to sit at table with a German.

'Isn't Hitler a fool! He thinks he can win the war against the Russians!'

He spoke quite loudly, his words must have been audible at least at the two neighbouring tables, and Prague was full of Gestapo men and informers. I begged him to speak more quietly.

'Why, don't you agree he's a fool?' he inquired, quite unabashed.

Sämisch lasted until 1944, then, when he had held forth in Madrid at the final banquet of a tournament, they nabbed him at the German frontier and shoved him into a concentration camp for a few months.

In April 1946 when we met in Switzerland, I asked how it had been in the camp.

'Incredible, nothing whatever to smoke!' And he added: 'What's worse, now I'm completely broke.' He never has any money—on principle. Legends are told about that. Once, to everyone's surprise, he spent some prize money on a typewriter with the intention of starting work. Next day, however, he decided he felt no desire to work, so he sold the machine at half the purchase price.

At the Easter tournament I also met the Prague chessmaster Dietz. After beating him in an interesting game, I got into conversation with him. Since he spoke Czech fluently and without any accent, I ventured to ask whether he had heard the news broadcast from London that the Germans had taken a beating again.

'No, I haven't heard it, but that's interesting, the war will soon be over,' he announced cheerfully.

At that moment Foltys dealt me a good kick from behind and, drawing me aside, whispered in some agitation:

'What do you think you're doing? Dietz is in the SS, he works at Gestapo headquarters.'

My blood ran cold. All evening I waited for the knock on the door but none came. Dietz was very friendly next day and we chatted about chess.

In May 1945 I learnt two things. First, that Dietz had saved a number of people from arrest—twenty-three had confirmed the fact in writing. Second, that he was now in a Russian prisoner-of-war camp, threatened with execution. I hastened to write a statement, which several Czech chess players signed, and Bedřich Thelen—with whom I had also played for the first time in 1943 when I learnt that he was a communist and former chairman of the Federation of Proletarian Physical Training—rushed to negotiate with the camp commander. Ultimately, Dietz was released and was even allowed to stay in Czechoslovakia instead of being transferred to Germany. When I was working in the trade unions I tried to help him find a job, but no one was willing to take on a German, except for hard manual labour—he would get beaten up they said. In the end, he decided to go to Germany rather than live among people who regarded him as only half human.

A letter and a postcard arrived from West Germany. I wrote twice, but no reply came. Years later I learnt that Dietz had been the victim of some kind of vengeance murder. What a horrifying fate! He could not live among Czechs because he was German, and he lived only briefly among the Germans because he had been good to Czechs.

About half way through the tournament, the Czech papers started writing about me as a sensational discovery. But the close was not so glorious. As was to be expected, Alekhine and Keres beat me, apparently in quite interesting games, but to a youngster only the games he wins seem interesting. I lost, too, to the third victor, Katetov, and to a less dangerous opponent, Urbanec. But my worst mishap came with the Austrian, Lokvenc. Playing a variation I had swotted up, I hardly looked at the board and in place of a correct seventh move, I made the eighth, which cost me a piece. After a bare five minutes' play, I had to resign. There was one good thing about it—we took a walk in lovely weather, and I liked the kindly Lokvenc so much that I invited him to partake of Mr. Stork's salami which, in any case, was so enormous that it was in danger of going bad.

My final placing as tenth out of twenty-one was generally regarded as a great success. Alekhine gave me high praise in the *Frankfurter Zeitung*, and during the closing ceremony I received an invitation to make a trip to the Reich. The prizes were presented by the Prime Minister of the Protectorate Government, and chessmaster Erhart Post, chairman of the Deutsche Schachbund and the Europa Schachbund, came from Berlin to deliver the speech. He praised the Czechs and their chess players, and also golden Prague, without a word about the New Europe or final victory. Then the prizewinners went forward, bowed, and Post shook them by the hand. But two of the Czech masters stood to attention, clicked their heels and raised their right arms in the Nazi salute. Let one be forgiven, he is dead. The other is politically in good favour today and, in 1971, when my case was being debated in the Chess Union, he replied to a suggestion that Pachman could, perhaps, be allowed to play in home competitions by declaring that such a step could not be reconciled with true communist principles.

Be that as it may, Mr. Post summoned me after the ceremony and, in the presence of two or three people, he said how much he had liked my play and he invited me to a tournament in Germany. Quite overcome, I stammered something about having to take exams and start a job, perhaps some time after the war. He understood. Saying in German, very good, good luck, he politely let me go. Apparently he was a Nazi, but a decent person none the less. I heard that he saved the German chess organization from being swallowed up by the ill-famed *Kampf durch Freude*.

A smaller tournament followed the Easter event, with Sämisch and Thelen among the well-known masters playing. Firmly resolved not to lose this opportunity, I sent a telegram to my headmaster that I was staying on. And on this occasion I won all rounds—out of eleven games I allowed just one opponent a draw, and that when victory was already in the bag. The road to a career in chess was open. In the autumn of that year, I placed third at the championship tournament in Zlin, and a year later I won the official title of chessmaster.

2. The Nazi Occupation

I first showed political interest at the age of nine. On May Day I saw a procession in the street. There was a beautiful red flag, banners flying, and people shouting, so I joined in, and copied what the others were doing—clenched fist, shouts of 'Down with the capitalists' and, the most popular, 'Open up the factory, Dobeš to prison!' Dobeš, I knew, was director of the local factory and obviously a fool because in the holidays I had been obliged to act as companion to his son and another boy from a wealthy family, and with young Dobeš I had come to blows right away. I was delighted with the idea that the father of this fathead should be put inside, so I supported the demand with a will.

At home I got a beating for my pains, followed by a lecture on Bolshevism. My father belonged to the right-wing National Unification Party. He cursed Beneš and welcomed the change next door in Germany.

Three years later violent arguments broke out at home over the Spanish Civil War. My brother Vladimír was very left wing, so he cursed Franco, while I enjoyed myself by cutting in with remarks directed now against the right, now against the left. My father let it pass, but Vladimír boxed my ears, and consequently, I responded by sympathizing with Franco.

Not until the spring of 1938 did I finally go over to my brother's side. During the May mobilization against Hitler's threat, I got mixed up in a demonstration. Vladimír stood up in the town square to declare that the Communists would defend the Republic, whereupon our local militiaman, Mr. Šafránek, rushed up crying: 'Mr. Pachman, move on this minute!' But people backed Vladimír, and he stood firm. And I was terribly proud that my brother was a public speaker.

I remember Munich very well. First I was involved in a demonstration where people yelled: 'We want a military dictatorship! Long live General Syrový!' Having no idea what a dictatorship was, I was enthusiastic because it was obviously something against the Germans.

Then, one morning, our class teacher stood before us. He was authorized by the headmaster to announce that. . . . He stopped in the middle and burst into tears. I was somehow more sorry for him than about the loss of our border districts, and I vowed never to tease him any more.

On 15 March 1939, I stayed away from school. As I watched the German troops arriving, one comical scene cheered me. A diminutive German officer was leading a squad of our soldiers to the place where they had to hand in their arms. A man in the front rank seemed to slip, his foot struck the officer, who fell flat on his back. I laughed uproariously; then it occurred to me that perhaps all was not lost if a soldier could manage to fell an officer of the occupying army so neatly.

I learnt from Vladimír that we were not going to give in, we would fight, but he refused to say how, because I was too dumb anyhow, and I talked too much.

Towards the end of November we got a letter saying that Vladimír had been arrested and taken off somewhere. That the universities had been closed we knew from the papers. His landlady told us the rest—about the student demonstration on 17 November, the shooting, the funeral of Jan Opletal who was killed that day, and the execution of nine other student leaders. The Gestapo and the Czech militia had burst into the colleges picking up everyone they could lay hands on. Vladimír's landlady had urged him to go back home at once, but he insisted he must attend a meeting of his faculty committee next day. The building was occupied by the Germans, and the guard first refused to admit him, but Vladimír declared it was academic soil, so he must be allowed in. Finally they let him go in, but they didn't let him go home for over three years.

I hadn't the faintest idea in those days what a concentration camp was, so I was extremely proud that my brother was in one.

I talked about it everywhere, and of course I was indignant. I used to write to him when he was in Sachenhausen. One had to write in German, which was a good exercise, and occasionally I received a reply. His letters were usually optimistic and I did not realize at the time that the words, 'I'm very well', were a necessary formality.

In August 1940, I went to the cinema with a school friend, Franta Kreibich. I can recall the film exactly—it was a German detective story, 'The Sixth Man Is Missing'. Instead of the newsreel, they put an announcement on the screen that 'shots from the battle fronts are not, for technical reasons, being shown.' I started clapping loudly, shouting 'Bravo, hurrah!' Franta was the first to join in, followed by the entire audience. We were all in a happy mood when we settled down to watch how the sixth man was unable to appear because he had been murdered.

Next day, around ten in the morning, the militiaman, Mr. Šafránek, arrived at our house to say I was to go along with him, some gentlemen wanted to talk to me. He chatted on the way saying nothing about the matter in hand. At the police station, however, in the presence of two strangers, he started lecturing me about the Reich, about obedience and so on. Having stopped him rather crossly, the gentlemen brought in Franta and drove us to a house in Mladá Boleslav. There we were received by a more important gentleman, in whose presence we had to stand to attention. He started questioning me—name, date of birth, father, followed by more interesting questions:

'You have a brother?'

I assented that that was true.

'Where is he?'

'In Sachenhausen concentration camp.'

'Well, you'll soon be seeing him!'

His tone was threatening, so remembering encounters with my teachers, I assumed a stupid expression and said:

'Really? You're letting him come home?'

He flew at me, dealing one blow from the right, another from the left to restore my balance, and I realized too late that there was no joking as with the teachers. Grabbing me by my shirt, he set

22

to banging my head against the wall, which was not particularly painful, but it made me drunk somehow.

When he let go of me, he turned to Franta, while I gradually collected my wits enough to listen to what would follow. In reply to the question why he had clapped in the cinema, Franta spoke quite confidently—evidently he was prepared. When we got to the cinema, he said, he found his shoelace was untied. Just when he was tying it, and therefore not looking at the screen, he heard me clapping and shouting 'Bravo!' Unaware of what it was about, he joined in.

That struck me as being an awfully silly excuse, so I was not at all sorry for him when he got slapped in the face—in any case, the blows were more in the nature of a bureaucratic exercise. Then they took us off to the local prison, emptied our pockets and put each of us in a different cell.

My cell was fairly spacious, about 9 by 15 feet, on one side a table and chair, on the other a bunk with a carefully folded blanket, and a flush lavatory in the corner. The warder, a Czech, briefly explained the prison regulations to me and left me alone.

The days passed terribly slowly. Apart from an hour's exercise every morning, when about fifty of us walked round and round the courtyard, there was nothing to do. So I tore the brown toilet paper they provided into squares. Then I applied for pen and paper, and when writing a letter home I managed to draw chess men on the squares and a board on the table. Having no one to play with, I tried to play against myself, but that was a wash-out because I knew my opponent's intentions, and the result was always a draw. One can tell from Zweig's *Schachnovelle* that the author never tried this method. Then I remembered how my brother used to compose chess problems, so I tried my hand at that. About three of my problems were later published and for one I got an 'honourable mention' in a competition.

Interrogations were a welcome distraction. They would put six or seven of us into a Black Maria for the drive to the Gestapo villa. They would ask about things at school, to which I replied that everyone was good and nobody complained. They didn't really believe me, but they left it at that. Twice they asked why I had clapped. By now I had my excuse ready—I had been looking forward to the detective film so much that I was glad I would be able to see it without delay. The interrogator wrote down my reply and made no objection. He was milder than the first one. Once he told me that they would not have taken me in, the Czech militia had done it—it was really rather silly.

When about a month had passed, they took us out again, this time to the baths. Franta and I were shut up there for a couple of hours, puzzling what it could mean. I suggested they might be listening to hear whether we would betray a secret, but no secret occurred to me. Finally we were taken before the interrogator who told us we could go home, but if we failed to conduct ourselves as good citizens of the Reich, we would find ourselves inside again. Next day, at 2.00 p.m. precisely, we were to report to the German militia in the town of Jičín—a mere formality, it seemed.

At school next day, I went straight to the headmaster; rather nervously I asked if I would be allowed to continue my studies. Mr. Kraus replied in his genial, deep bass:

'Do you know, in September a gentleman from the Gestapo rang to say I was to expel you. I told him it would be difficult, because Pachman had not presented himself for registration at the beginning of the school year. How could I expel him if he was not a pupil here? Well now, just go to your classroom, maybe the gentleman will forget about it.'

Not a word of rebuke. It dawned on me that this was a good man whom I should not annoy as I used to. I had little chance to carry out my resolution. Before the year was out, there was a big round-up of officials of the Sokol physical training movement—headmaster Kraus never returned from concentration camp.

I stayed at school; they really had forgotten about me. But Franta's headmaster was not so good. He gave him a lecture about the Reich before expelling him.

The Gestapo took it out on us the day after our return, however. The formality of reporting in Jičín turned into a gruelling two hours on the parade ground to teach us 'the positive attitude to work required of all citizens of the Reich'. We ended up being made to crawl three times round the ground in a state of utter exhaustion.

3. With the Victorious Army

■.

Still at school, I studied chess diligently and dreamt of being world champion. Some exercises I sent to *Deutsche Schachblätter* were published with a note, at my request, that they were 'dedicated to my brother'. I sent copies to Vladimír in the concentration camp—he was allowed to receive German newspapers and magazines.

He wrote: 'I was happy about the news from home, especially about Luděk's trip.' I glowed with pride. It is praise indeed to meet with approval from a brother six years one's senior.

At school there were incessant debates about the eastern front. Things looked bad at first, until we heard the news about the German disaster outside Moscow. Then, in the summer of 1942, the lads decided the Bolsheviks were done for, but I stubbornly maintained that Stalingrad would not fall. And at the very time when the Führer had written off his heroes in that city, and the radio was broadcasting funeral fanfares, we heard that Vladimír had been released. After taking my school-leaving examination in June, I moved to Prague to live with him in his lodgings.

In the summer of 1943 he gave me a little book to read. It was called *Ludwig Feuerbach and the End of Classical German Philosophy*. It was pretty hard going. I asked questions now and then and was surprised that matter is in continuous motion. Engels's *Dialectics of Nature* followed, which I found most interesting. I began to think myself very wise, and that I understood the world and life. A few more books convinced me about the need for class struggle, and then, finally, I read the famous slogan, 'Workers of all lands, unite!'

I would have united forthwith, but with whom? Vladimír evidently had some contacts, but he refused to let me in on anything

26

—I talked too much and just wasn't suited for such things. But one day in the early summer of 1944 he asked if I could hold my tongue; it was a matter of life or death. Someone would be staying for a few days in his room. He would go to friends and tell our landlady that the visitor was a cousin. So a young man moved in with me. He was out most of the time, but in the evenings we sometimes talked a bit. When the war was over, I learnt that he was the Commissar of the Jan Svoboda Partisan Regiment. When our landlady got to know in May 1945, at first she accused us of nearly landing her on the gallows, but soon she calmed down and the whole street knew that she had bravely given shelter to a partisan commander.

In February 1945 several chessmasters and chess officials met together in Karel Opočenský's flat. We discussed how to reorganize our Chess Union, how to get in touch with the Soviet players, and altogether how to go ahead after the war. One idea was to hold regular Prague-Moscow matches. The first match was, in fact, held early in 1946, but it was also the last.

At the conclusion of our 'illegal' meeting Opočenský regaled us from his hidden store of brandy. Altogether he was well supplied because he made a habit in those days of playing simultaneous matches for payment solely in flour, eggs or pork. On his birthday there was a real feast, with a fat goose—one of the best happenings in the whole war except that the goose was the cause of lifelong enmity between Opo and chessmaster Richter. It was like this: in January 1945, I decided the time had come to have another tournament, and since no one else wanted to organize it, I took on the job. Among people from whom I collected money was Mr. Stork, who also promised a first prize in the shape of a fat goose. Six masters met in a two-round tournament. Opo was in top form, leading two rounds before the end by $1\frac{1}{2}$ points over Richter and myself. So, full of confidence, he approached Mr. Stork to let him have the prize goose for his birthday party. That was a week before the tournament ended.

However, as luck would have it, Opo lost both his games. I won one and drew one, Richter won two. Opo tactfully excused himself from the prize-giving ceremony—Richter inquired about

27

the goose. A terrible row ensued. Anxious though he was to save the situation, Mr. Stork was powerless to provide another goose, so he presented Richter with a hen, a chicken and a hare. But those two never made it up, they always avoided each other at tournaments and when obliged to play each other, they refused to shake hands.

When Prague Radio announced the approach of the liberating armies, I was at home with my parents. Brushing aside my father's strict injunction to stay put, I rushed out to join people gathering in the streets. We started to discuss what to do, chiefly the setting up of a revolutionary national committee—someone had heard that this was the correct name. Who should head it? The obvious man for the job was Mr. Bina, head of the co-op, and prewar chairman of the local Communist Party. So we crowded into his shop. But Mr. Bina greeted us with undisguised reluctance—he had no time, he objected, he had to weigh out sugar. It struck me as incredible that the revolution should be held up on account of sugar, and I made no bones about saying so. Mr. Bina stood firm, however, whereupon we decided to make the revolution without him.

People were standing about in groups; at first no German soldiers were to be seen, but then we noticed a machine-gun post in the park, and the school entrance was blocked by sandbags. We held a meeting on the empty ground floor of a house on the edge of the town square. Having weighed up the situation, we came to the conclusion that for accomplishing the revolution we had at our disposal two official-issue militia revolvers and three hunting rifles—clearly inadequate for coping with the machine guns of the local garrison.

We were still debating when suddenly—crash, and then rat-tat-tat—a window shattered and someone yelled: 'SS!'

Without a thought for the two revolvers and three hunting rifles, we made for the courtyard, across it to a garden and, climbing or rolling over the fence, we chased down to the stream, only coming to a halt when we reached the woods. About an hour later a self-styled courier brought us the news that, while we were meeting, people standing around in the square had been saying that we were discussing revolution. A German must have telephoned to Mladá Boleslav, whence came two armoured cars and two troop-carriers full of SS men, who hastened to throw a hand-grenade and fire a volley from their tommy guns at our house. Luckily, they thought we were armed, and by the time they had deployed to take the place by storm we were safely in the woods.

When all was quiet we went home to sleep. In the morning, we found that the German Commissar had vacated the Town Hall, so we placed a Czechoslovak flag on it and held our meeting right there. Not far away, the school still showed the swastika— in short, dual power.

On the fourth day of the revolution we were patrolling the main street and I was leaning on a rifle which I still had not really learnt to use, when someone shouted 'Germans!' Before I had time to run, tanks, cars, a flood of Germans were clattering around me. I wanted at least to hide the rifle, but something incredible was happening—from the tanks and lorries, tommy guns, revolvers, rifles were flying in our direction; the army was surrendering to us! Hastily assuming an air of importance, I slung my rifle casually over my shoulder and started gathering up the weaponry. The army continued its journey to the south-west, where it sensed the American presence.

We mobilized reserves to help pile up the booty in the Sokol hall. I selected a light Italian automatic, a revolver and three hand-grenades. Recruits came in gradually, most of them boys I knew from school. A captain in Czechoslovak uniform assumed command—he must have treasured the uniform all through the war in readiness for this moment. Běla had its army.

We heard that near the station, in the direction of my chess village, Čistá, something terrible had happened. Four boys had fired from a distance at a German convoy; some of the soldiers had gone back to the woods where the boys were hiding, caught them unawares, and within a few minutes all four had been executed by hanging. Immediately, we occupied all the approaches to the town, placed the machine guns and dug holes for the bazookas. Then we had to have a trial run. Volleys from submachine-guns and detonating hand-grenades threw the town into a panic—people dived for the cellars. A courier came running to find out what was up and we were firmly told to stop the nonsense.

Later, under protest, we had to move into the woods, because SS men were reported to be advancing on the town. They failed to turn up, but we kept guard into the night. I was wearing a German helmet on which I had stuck a red star bought at the stationer's. The shopkeeper had organized production very promptly —as yet there was no planning to hold things up. I must have looked pretty terrifying. Seeing a youngster in German uniform in a field, I popped out of the bushes crying *'Hände hoch!'*, whereupon he briskly hit the ground and started screaming quite hysterically. Approaching him with my best German, I told him to shut up, I wouldn't bite him. Still terrified, he sat up and started to tell me something, but I simply gave him directions for the retreat route. He marched, or rather scuttled away, probably wondering how such an enormous red star could let him go.

We were standing next morning on the corner by the Sokol house when someone spread the news that the Russians were coming. People rushed up to assist in the welcome. After some confusion about the direction from which to expect them, we stood ready to shout, but—we gazed dumbfounded, for down the road came horse-drawn carts, an old chap on each horse, and on the carts, hay and some sacks. Now and then the old chaps cracked their whips, the horses pulled and the carts jolted past us. What sort of an army was this? Was this the way to defeat the Germans?

Some twenty carts went by, then all was quiet. Nobody spoke, we just felt disappointed.

About half an hour later, we heard a loud racket, a giant tank loomed round the corner, its treads skidded on the bend, the tank reared and turned into the main road—now, at last, we broke into a roar, and soon we were welcoming a second, third, fourth of the famous T34s.

At midday a column halted by the Town Hall and the officers went inside for an official welcome. Obviously, the revolution was over. I asked the crew of a troop carrier if they would take me to Prague. Ivan waved me up, but before I mounted he took that excellent Italian automatic off me. Luckily I had the revolver out of sight in my rucksack. Soon we were on our way, with me sitting none too comfortably on an enormous heap of peas. But people along the road waved and shouted hurrah, and since my two companions made no response, I cried hurrah as if on behalf of the victorious allied army.

All went well until we met another tank coming out of a side-road. Our driver swerved, so we ran into the ditch and over-turned, with the result that I was buried so deep in peas they had to pull me out.

Finally, I got a lift on a Czech lorry to the outskirts of Prague, and from there I completed the journey on foot. By the time I reached the city centre, it was dark. People were standing around, some waiting for soup to be handed out, others running about on some business or other. Being famished, I accepted an offering of potato cakes. Then I slept for some fifteen hours in our old landlady's house.

In the morning I remembered it was my birthday, but how to celebrate? I went into the streets. Nearby I saw a notice—Communist Party of Czechoslovakia, District Office. I entered and said, 'Good morning. Please can you tell me how I can join your party?' They had no time, I should write my application on a piece of paper. So I took a piece of paper and wrote that I was in favour of world revolution and socialism, so I wished to apply for membership in the Communist Party.

4. The Central Trade Union Council

▪▪▪▪▪▪▪▪▪▪▪▪▪▪▪▪▪▪▪▪▪▪▪▪▪▪▪▪▪▪▪▪▪▪▪

So now the war was over and I finished writing a pamphlet about the six-masters' tournament.

We had great plans for chess. Aware that in the Soviet Union the state looked after the organization of the game, we felt that by pointing to this model it would be child's play to achieve the spread of chess throughout our country. We drafted a plan of action, and the same day three of us betook ourselves to the key institutions: the Ministry of Education, the Central Trade Union Council and the Youth League. Each of us would first point to the example of the Soviet Union, and then maintain that the other two bodies had already included chess in their programmes. Possibly, in the general confusion of those days, we would get away with it!

The trade unions fell to me, because my brother, as it happened, was working there in the cultural department. But I needed to talk to his boss. At first the secretary allowed me access only to his deputy, but I must have made a good impression because he passed me on to an office more luxurious than any I had ever set eyes upon. I was greeted by a lively, baldish gentleman who addressed me as comrade. I found difficulty in adopting the familiar form of address, so I spoke quite impersonally while expatiating on the remarkable educational value of chess. My efforts were crowned with unexpected success:

'If you want to work here, you can start at once, or would you rather wait till Monday?'

Although I had really intended to study and make some sort of living out of chess, the luxurious office was tempting. I decided to start at once in case he changed his mind.

32

My job was to organize chess groups in industrial and other concerns. Things went pretty well, but to be on the safe side I made a point of multiplying the number of new groups by three when making my reports, to avoid chess getting lost among all the other cultural activities.

The department secretary interested me. Her name was Euženie and I gathered she had been in a fighting unit, which impressed me enormously. On various excuses, I used to visit her office, but further than that I dared not go. Then, in January 1946, there was a discussion about who should represent our department at the Lenin anniversary celebration. Nobody was keen to go; they all had a heap of work. In the end the chief briskly solved the matter by deciding that his secretary should go, and I, being the youngest member of the staff, should accompany her. On hearing that, I hastily swallowed the excuse I had prepared.

We sat that evening in a box, we listened to a speech, some recitations, some singing, and more talk—a programme lasting over three hours, which was very exhausting. As it happened, I had some meat coupons, so afterwards I made so bold as to invite Euženie to a restaurant for supper. When the waiter offered me a bottle of special apricot brandy, I dared not ask the price, but I trembled to think that the bill might be more than I could pay. However, all went well and we got on famously. As we walked home, I took Euženie's arm, we stood on a bridge where I talked about the stars and kissed her. At that moment, it seems, I looked quite a man of the world, but that was due to the apricot brandy.

After that I visited the Smíchov district of Prague, where Euženie lived, almost every day. We would go to a favourite inn for a small black beer—I had to economize financially after that bottle of brandy—but most of the time we walked the streets, stopping in the alcoves of the old houses.

In April our chess team travelled to Switzerland for a tournament. The trip was organized by the trade union centre, meaning myself. I arranged with some skill that Euženie accompanied us as secretary, and the chief, who knew nothing until the last moment, was surprised that I had stolen his secretary.

Things were lively in Prague on our return. The first post-war elections were approaching. We walked the streets, tearing down Czech Socialist posters and replacing them with our own, the Communist—but not for long, because the Socialists were quick to retaliate.

Once, as I was passing the 'National House' in Smíchov, I saw a poster advertising an election meeting to be addressed by a lady Member of Parliament for the Catholic People's Party; the speech to be followed by questions and discussion. The word discussion fascinated me, so I went right in, took a seat near the front, and listened to the lady. She spoke about democracy: she was not against socialism, but the Communists, she said, were out to get power for themselves and something had to be done to prevent them. When my turn came in the discussion, I got down to work. There was a bit of a stir, then two robust stewards half-pushed, half-carried me out of the hall. A few people who protested at this treatment followed me out, so, taking up a position by the cloakroom, I delivered a brief speech, which provoked a few comments, but most of my audience agreed with me.

Annoyed by the lady speaker, I resolved to get my own back. Taking as my target an article she had published in 'Horizon', her party's paper, where she maintained that things are never black and white—'why, even Hitler loved his dog'—I wrote a fine essay on the theme that love of dogs could not compensate for the millions slaughtered in concentration camps. In my ardour, I failed to notice that the lady had suggested nothing of the kind. Then I took a dislike to one of the editors of the Catholic paper, Pavel Tigrid, whose articles were intelligent, but they struck me as too clever by half. I had a go at him, too, in our paper, 'People's Culture', and was surprised to find no response in 'Horizon'. Now, years later, Pavel Tigrid tells me that he never read our paper. Probably nobody read it, only trade union officials bought it as a duty. In any case, I have often blushed to think of my journalistic beginnings, especially when we in Prague would eagerly scan *Svědectví*, the paper Tigrid publishes abroad, even copying and passing on some of the articles.

I was out of the country for the elections because we were in Moscow playing the match we had planned in February 1945. During the summer I visited Euženie regularly. Soon we began to talk of marriage, but first we wanted to find a place of our own. I hunted around, but all in vain. In my simplicity it never occurred to me to use the political influence summed up by the slogan, 'The Central Trade Union Council—a Great Power', but there is no reason for me to boast about that, the idea simply never entered my head.

Early in September, I suddenly resolved that the wedding must take place immediately, so I informed Euženie that the matter was settled. I rushed off to arrange the formalities. It was a Monday, and the only time the registry office could offer was Friday, 6 September, because nobody wanted to be married on that 'unlucky day'. Arranging for the banns to be waived was done within half an hour, but then we were told that we both had to present a certificate of citizenship. From the form they gave us I learnt that we would each need about thirty documents, including such things as our fathers' school reports from 1910. Some could be dealt with by making a declaration, but others had to be produced. On going through our papers, we found we could provide about one-fifth; to obtain the rest would take at least two months. Thoroughly annoyed by now, I grabbed all the papers and went to the National Committee (in other words, our local council office).

'Madam,' I said to the woman in the appropriate department, 'I am about to go abroad on an important business trip and I need to get married before I leave. Please can you give me the necessary documents at once?'

Glancing at my papers, she announced that it was impossible, but after further discussion she got rid of me by sending me upstairs to her department chief—if he proved willing, well and good.

Out in the corridor, I went round the corner and walked up and down for a while, then, returning to her room at a run, I announced breathlessly: 'Everything in order, I have the permission, you are to be so kind as to issue me the documents at once.'

The lady registered surprise, while I trembled that she might reach for the telephone. However, she started filling in the forms, pinning my miserable collection of documents to them. Then she handed the whole lot over, saying: 'Since the chief officer has given you permission, let him sign.'

When I got out of the room, I folded the documents to make them thicker, shoved them under the forms and betook myself to the chief's office.

'Sir, I am about to go abroad on business. Your assistant and I would be obliged if you would sign this.'

Without a glance at my documents, he signed the forms and I departed in triumph. Later many acquaintances told me that to get a certificate of citizenship was real martyrdom, but none ventured to imitate me.

The wedding was fixed for nine o'clock on the Friday morning. For a joke, we decided to say nothing at work, so at eight we turned up as usual. Eužcnie applied for leave to visit the dentist —I, being my own master, had no need to ask permission. As we were leaving, she asked me if I had a witness. That pulled me up short—what with the mad business of the documents one couldn't think of everything. Hastily I approached a bachelor colleague who, having heard my tale, refused because he was not dressed for the occasion and there was no time even to shave. Having tried persuasion, I now made a generous offer—for his services in this matter I would give him forty cigarettes. His resistance broken, he accompanied us, still grumbling, to the registry office. There they asked if we had a bouquet and again I had to confess that I had forgotten. With briefcases in our hands, we stood listening to the registrar's address, after which it transpired that I had forgotten the rings as well. We got them a year or two later. In short, an improvised wedding, with a feast of real goose on the following Sunday. Not until a quarter of a century later was the ceremony to acquire its true significance. Now, however, I had plenty of plans for the future. Some succeeded, others had to be dropped, but I shall never regret that day—when times have been hard I have valued it especially.

By then I was already speaking at Party meetings and holding an official position as chairman of a so-called cultural commission for three branches. The more responsible post of Party instructor at the Realist Theatre in Smíchov was also entrusted to me. There I made friends with the actors and I have been a loyal frequenter of their theatre for many years.

5. February 1948

■▪

In the autumn of 1947—it must have been October or November
—I learnt that something was afoot. A confidential Party document instructed us that 'it is necessary to be prepared for a
decisive encounter with the reactionaries before the elections'.
The elections were due in the spring of 1948. The official explanation was that, in a bid to forestall the anticipated Communist
victory at the polls, the reactionaries might attempt a coup.
People in the know, however, took the instructions to mean—the
fight is on. Veteran Communist Antonín Zápotocký, then chairman of the trade unions, helped the leader Klement Gottwald to
muster a 'people's militia' commanded by, and largely recruited
from, former partisan fighters.

The Communist Party had problems—goods were in short
supply and people were upset that, in this miserable situation,
Czechoslovakia had—on orders from Moscow—refused to join
in the Marshall Plan. The Communists proposed a 'millionaires'
levy' which, in view of the fact that little more than a year had
passed since the currency reform had frozen all assets, was something of a joke; it caused a big fuss, none the less. I was supposed
to speak somewhere on the subject, but the instructions about
what should be said seemed to me so feeble that I declined to
address that particular meeting.

In 1946 the Communist Party had won 38 per cent of the
votes, a success unprecedented in world history. The coming
elections were bound to register a decrease, and the 'people's
militia' on the streets would provide the answer to all obstacles—
the answer which was given in February 1948.

I observed those turbulent days from a distance because I
happened to be in hospital recovering from two operations.

Following events on a croaking radio set, I had a pretty good idea of the situation. When the non-Communist Ministers resigned from the Government, I remarked to my fellow patients that the move was crazy, they would simply drop out and gain nothing. Then events followed thick and fast. The trade unions called a congress of factory councils, a protest strike drew wide support, Gottwald presented President Beneš with an ultimatum—accept the resignations and let the Communist Party form a government or else! The alternative was clear: the militia was marching the streets and when President Beneš inquired of the Minister of Defence, General Ludvík Svoboda, whether the Army would intervene against the use of force, the Minister replied, 'The Army will not move against the people.'

Within a few years Svoboda received his reward—an unexpected one, but not unusual in our part of the world. First he was demoted to the post of Chairman of the State Office for Physical Training and Sport, then kicked out altogether. He worked on a co-operative farm in south Bohemia until, one fine day in 1955, the good Nikita Khrushchev, on a visit to Prague, inquired of his hosts: 'What is my old friend Svoboda doing?'

Consternation all round! A government car was hastily despatched to fetch Svoboda, a brand-new general's uniform was made within a matter of hours, and the old friends met in full glory. To return to 1948: for the second time in a decade, the President accepted resignations. Gottwald gave the news to the 100,000 people waiting in Prague's Old Town Square. Militiamen and other Party members cheered vociferously—our radio set at the hospital nearly fell to pieces. Luckily on that occasion, at least, I was not present, for I too would have cheered.

Shortly after the glorious victory I was discharged from hospital, but with two legs in plaster I had to stay at home for several weeks. Action Committees, so I heard, were being set up everywhere, their job being to put things in order, chase out reactionaries wherever they were to be found and ensure our advance by leaps and bounds to socialism. I received notification of my appointment to the post of general secretary of the Action Committee of CUCC (Central Union of Czechoslovak Chess-

39

players) and was entrusted with the task of cleansing this socially important institution. The Chairman was a figurehead—one of the non-Communist politicians who had decided to collaborate. At the very first meeting it was obvious that the decisions would be up to me. I had received confidential instructions about who was to be expelled; in the first place, officials and members of the non-Communist parties who remained active and, having failed to recognize the error of their ways, refused to co-operate with the new régime.

Obviously this applied first and foremost to Josef Louma, an enthusiastic chessmaster who had long served as an official of our organization. He had immediately been dismissed following the February events from his post as director of a big Prague factory because he was a member of the Beneš Party. True, he and I had often engaged in heated political debates, but to debate and to throw a man out seemed to me to be quite different matters. So, pushing aside the confidential instructions, I moved that: 'All officials of CUCC have manifested their loyalty to the people's democratic order, therefore we consider the purging of our organization to have been accomplished. Anyone against?' It was not the custom in those days to be against, so the motion was carried and a report sent to the appropriate quarters. However, not long after we had a letter from the Central Action Committee—it had been established, etc., etc., and the final sentence: 'Josef Louma to be dismissed from all public positions.'

What now? It occurred to me that with all that was happening, a little thing like this might be overlooked. Laying aside the letter with the earlier instructions, I said nothing. To my surprise, however, Opočenský asked at the next meeting, as if by the way, whether any instructions had come about Louma, to which I replied that correspondence was my business, he need not worry about it. A week later I was called to the Central Action Committee to be told that Opočenský had called attention to the matter of Louma. During a sharp argument, I proffered my resignation, but in the end they calmed down, leaving it to me to decide what to do, but 'something had to be done.'

I arranged matters quite successfully. Another man was nominated, *pro forma*, as a member of our committee, while Louma remained in the capacity of paid secretary—since he was out of work, with no prospect of finding another job in chess. Subsequently he also joined the editorial staff of 'Czechoslovak Chess'. But I was able to report 'to the top' that he had been demoted to 'a position of lesser importance'. We remained friends until his death in 1955; occasionally we quarrelled about politics, but never again in public. With Opo, however, friendship was at an end.

6. Educating the Workers

■▪■▪■▪■▪■▪■▪■▪■▪■▪■▪■▪■▪■▪■▪■▪■▪■▪■▪■▪■

On my return to work, I was transferred to a new job: that of organizing 'mass education'. The idea was to arrange courses in factories and offices to promote the rapid spread of Marxist views among the trade union membership. I engaged in drawing up study plans, writing lecture notes, calling meetings and travelling around the country.

President Beneš resigned at the end of May and in September he died. After February he had been praised for his statesman-like wisdom; now, at a meeting of our Party branch, a speaker 'from the centre' damned him completely. I objected that it was unseemly to praise a public man during his life, then to damn him as soon as he was dead. That started a big debate, followed by a special meeting a week later to settle our differences. Another member of our department joined me in drafting a motion deploring the offensive words about Dr. Beneš and also sharply attacking the so-called Gottwald appeal (a campaign compelling office workers, teachers and many others to apply for Communist Party membership).

We had a stormy meeting. Several of the old Party men opposed me; my brother gesticulated, shouting: 'Comrades, do you realize you are going against the Party's general line?'

The motion was carried, none the less, and despatched to Party headquarters. The response was an attack on me at our next meeting made by our district secretary on behalf of the Central Committee. He started boldly, accusing me of dangerous intellectualism, but we soon had him red in the face, until, in the midst of the debate, he announced that he was pressed for time, grabbed his hat and literally ran away. Long after I learnt that my case had been the subject of investigation at headquarters,

42

but although I was found to have some intellectualist leanings, my loyalty to the working class was regarded as impeccable. Nothing more came of the affair.

Early in 1949 our department head—a most kindly, but utterly incompetent man, who was incapable of putting words together so that to hear him address a meeting was an outright tragedy— had a violent quarrel with a trade union official. An hour later I was summoned to the Council to hear the surprising news that I had been appointed head of the central department for trade union education. At the age of twenty-five it was my job to educate the working class in the spirit of the great ideas of Marxism-Leninism and proletarian internationalism.

Naturally, my first step was to reorganize the department, nearly doubling its size. I planned to establish a network of well-staffed schools for trade union officials. Despite staffing diffi-culties (I took the bold step of bringing in university graduates), I soon had under central management twenty-six schools, with several hundred teachers and administrative staff. At first I worked with enthusiasm, but in the course of time certain things began to worry me—the quarrels in the trade union leadership, for instance, where two groups squabbled over minor matters, while the major issues were decided by the Communist Party.

Month after month we lectured, thought up syllabuses, wrote resolutions, made tours of inspection. We lived in a world of our own, in our narrow circle, unaware of what was really happening in the country. While we were busy educating— churning out phrases about the evils of exploitation and the happy future before us—tens of thousands were being thrown into prison, hundreds of thousands robbed of their livelihood. Small tradesmen were deprived of the modest means scraped to-gether by the efforts of past generations, hard-working farmers whose forebears had, by the sweat of their brows, gradually en-larged their holdings, were labelled as 'kulaks' (rich farmers) and driven from their homes like cattle. No one told me about these things because the persecuted had no faith in us, the Commun-ists. It may seem hard to believe that I knew nothing, but, un-fortunately, that is the truth.

But ignorance is no excuse. Occasional reports in the news-papers should have made one think. There was the commotion about the 'Čihošť miracle', for instance. Father Toufar, a village priest, was alleged to have installed a simple mechanism by means of which he caused the statue of a saint to move during Mass, thereby staging a miracle. I saw the cinema newsreel showing the priest's hand pulling the wire, and in conclusion we were told he would receive the punishment he deserved. Why did I accept the story? Would it really have been possible to film a fake miracle in church without people knowing? Moreover, Father Toufar was never brought to trial—we should have asked what had happened. But for that we had no thought as we held forth about revolution, social justice and the power of the working class.

Not until 1968 did I learn the true story. Having installed the mechanism in the church, the security police then 'discovered' it. They planned a big trial at which the sinister role of religion would be unmasked. The plan foundered on a detail. Despite persistent torture, Father Toufar refused to confess, he was resolved to tell the truth in court. The job of the interrogator, Mácha, was to extract a confession, but he beat his victim to death. Mácha has never had to answer for his deed; he acted 'on Party instructions'.

In due course, with the help of experts from the Soviet Union, interrogation methods were improved; then everyone confessed —to espionage, sabotage, subversion. Reading the newspapers, we marvelled how many criminals there were among us. Three 'ecclesiastical trials' ended in three death sentences, plus a number of ten-, fifteen- and twenty-year terms of imprisonment. Dr. Trochta, now a Cardinal, spent four years in Dachau con- centration camp under the Nazis, and eleven years in a 'socialist prison'. A woman Member of Parliament, Dr. Milada Horáková, was executed. Why did none of us protest?

On one occasion when, at a Party meeting, we were being told about the crimes committed by Otto Šling, I said it seemed to me that while some things appeared to be true, others were surely exaggerated. I thought it improbable, for instance, that he had killed his mother by an injection. When this mild comment was greeted with horror, I realized that people were afraid. I was not afraid, therefore I cannot plead that as an excuse—I was merely indifferent to matters which failed to tally with the maxims of our faith.

Early in 1950 I was asked to write an article about trade union education. My manuscript was returned by the editors of the journal concerned with the comment: 'This article contains suitable quotations from the works of Marx, Lenin, Comrades Stalin and Gottwald, but it would be in place to add a suitable quotation from Comrade Slánský.' No problem, I had our research department at my service. The article duly appeared with the Slánský quotation.

Shortly after, Comrade Slánský delivered a public statement of self-criticism, announcing that he would continue to work devotedly for the Party in the lesser post of Deputy Prime Minister (previously he had been General Secretary of the Communist Party). Six months later Slánský was comrade no more, he was a traitor, painted by the press in the likeness of a foul reptile. In due course we listened to the broadcast of the great show trial at which he and the other defendants confessed to all manner of crimes and demanded that severe punishment be meted out to them.

I was losing faith by then, but I had not yet lost it completely. The atmosphere of suspicion disgusted me, however. When I received two or three reports denouncing members of my staff as agents of the traitor Slánský, I told my secretary they must be the work of unbalanced minds, and I threw them into the waste basket. Then I too was denounced.

The occasion was a visit in company with another trade union official to our chairman who, though a sick man at the time, insisted on managing affairs from his bed in the VIP sanatorium. Thrusting a sheaf of papers into my hand, he cried in a quavering voice: 'Read that aloud!'

It was a ten-page letter from the headmaster of one of our trade union schools, revealing that I was a member of the Slánský gang. His evidence was to the effect that I rejected workers in favour of intellectuals when making staff appointments. Furthermore, he detailed the points where I had deviated from the teachings of Marx, Engels, Lenin and Stalin in my efforts to introduce into our trade union movement theories of reformism, revisionism, social democracy and Zionism.

Comrade Chairman then cried in a loud voice: 'What do you say to that?'

I remarked that I had nothing much to say, the headmaster was obviously a fool and his ravings left me cold. At which I was treated to a long speech on trade union issues, the principles of Party vigilance and so on, concluding with the Chairman brandishing the letter as he exclaimed: 'If only a tenth of this is true, it's terrible!'

My companion tried to soothe him in honeyed tones, but when the door had closed behind us, he made a gesture of disgust.

Then I ran into trouble with the Party committee because a friend of mine, formerly head of our cultural department, had been sacked on suspicion of involvement with the traitor Slánský. When clearing out his desk, they found some notes I had written about life in the USSR—practical information to help him when he visited that country with a trade union delegation. Remarks such as: 'There is really nothing much to be bought: the best buys are vodka, cognac and black caviare. The best way to make some roubles is to speak for the Czech transmission of Moscow Radio—you can talk about nothing in particular and they pay well. Be prepared to have to go to the opera to see *Boris Godunov* and to the ballet, *Flames of Paris*—both terribly boring.' These were classified as disparaging and slanderous. Thanks to my journalistic work, however, I could demonstrate that I had never shown disrespect for the Soviet Union, so in the end it all blew over.

But these two episodes killed any interest I might have had in a political career. I resolved to get out. The problem was how to quit without being labelled a member of the 'anti-state centre'. While I was pondering the matter, an unexpected opportunity appeared.

The telephone rang: 'Comrade, Vice-Premier Kopecky will speak to you.'

This was way above my level, so at first I thought it was a hoax. But the phone started firing words like a machine-gun, convincing me that this was indeed the most powerful man after Gottwald, responsible equally with his boss for the murder of friends and colleagues. The voice went on and on, talking, for instance, about how we had been at the same school: 'No, Comrade Vice-Premier, those teachers were no longer there in my day', was about all I managed to get in. In about half an hour, he came to the point—the management of sport was to be reorganized, and he wanted my opinion whether chess should come under sport or culture; it would be best if I came to see him next day.

Having hastily conferred with the chess leadership, I was empowered to say we would prefer sport because we knew there would be more money there. It took a good two hours before the Minister got round to that, so I was almost on the way out before I could put in a quick word about my own business. I had to decide whether to carry on in politics or to devote myself to chess. Which did the comrade think I should choose? Naturally, I dished it up so he would think what suited me, and it worked. He actually thumped the table as he proclaimed: 'We've got dozens of stupid trade unionists, but only one chess player like you!' Grabbing the phone, he told someone at Party headquarters that I was to leave the trade union office. In addition to playing chess, I was to head the newly established chess section of the sports department, and the comrade was to arrange things accordingly.

Before the week was out I was asked to name my successor. I chose a young man from our central school. Then I gave notice to leave on 15 February 1953, and for a full fifteen years I dropped out of politics.

Now I started travelling the world, playing in tournaments, writing books. In those years I published twelve books on chess, and also occupied myself on the organizational side. Some things went well, some less well, but I always found the work much more interesting than politics.

Not that I had lost all interest—I was counted as an expert on political matters among my fellow chess players. In 1955 I heard something about the goings-on which later became known as 'the personality cult'. I spent a whole night during a tournament in Göteborg discussing these matters with the Dutch grandmaster, Donner. Holding strongly anti-Communist views at the time, he had decided not to play any matches in Eastern Europe. I told him what I knew and assured him that a big change was on the way—then we would see what socialism was really like; there would be no more jailing of dissenters; free speech and prosperity would reign because something would be done to cure our economic backwardness.

As dawn broke Donner was still sceptical, so I gave him a solemn promise: should things fail to improve in our country and the Communist movement prove incapable of building a new society, I would turn my back on it all; then I would fight the system to my last breath. The promise was made over the second bottle of brandy, but I have never forgotten it.

When, a few months later, Nikita Khrushchev spoke at the Twentieth Congress of the Soviet Communist Party, I was profoundly relieved. Now others would put things in order. There was no need for me to fight and I could play chess in peace.

7. International Chess

■.

Chess tournaments possess a magic all their own. It is hard to convey the atmosphere to those who have never played the game —even the occasional player will not really understand if he has not, at least, been able to watch a big event.

To play a tournament means to spend two, three or four weeks in utter concentration and breathless tension. Some players disguise their feelings during matches by assuming an air of indifference—having made a move, they walk about, examine their rivals' games, exchange a few words with the spectators. This happens usually during the first hours of play. Then comes the critical phase. The master remains seated at the board with the tense gaze of a hunter sighting his prey—that is, when he stands to win—or with the expression of a convict awaiting execution when things are going badly for him. Many players get red ears when they are losing, which serves as a danger signal for the wives who are not experts at the game.

Play usually lasts five hours, followed by an adjournment of the game until the next day. A game I played against the Yugoslav, Gligoric, in Moscow in 1947 occupied three sittings, a total of thirteen and a half hours. After 132 moves, Gligoric resigned, whereupon the only surviving spectator, who had stuck it out all through the difficult but boring endgame came up to tell me: 'You didn't beat him, you tortured him!'

He was quite right, and I remonstrated with the stewards when they wanted to eject the man.

I played an equally lengthy game in 1955, in Mar del Plata, this time without a break. That was because it was not uncommon in the Argentine in those days for deals to be done over adjourned games. Since in the last round of a tournament it is obvious who is likely to win the prize, games could be sold to whoever had the best chance. To prevent this a rule was made that the last round had to be played to the end. Competitors were not even allowed to leave the hall where they were under strict supervision by the judges.

On that occasion I was playing the great star of the Argentine, the young grandmaster, Panno. The game was vital for both of us but we were very tired, having been up till three in the morning at a reception given by the Mayor of Mar del Plata. The last round started at two in the afternoon and the organizers reckoned that all games would be finished by ten at the latest. The prizes were to be presented at a banquet, timed for ten-thirty. Punctually at that hour the official guests had gathered, the champagne was ready, the hors d'oeuvre on the plates. But Panno and I were still playing.

I had black. Having had to defend myself for a considerable time, I went over to counter-attack and after five hours of play the game could have been won in a single move. In the heat of the moment, however, I made a bad move, which led to a difficult endgame. With all the other games finished, the organizers were casting reproachful glances at us, as much as to say that we really might call it a day. But now the situation was delicate. I saw just one chance of winning. Before venturing on the decisive manoeuvre, however, I had to lull my opponent into a sense of security because a really precise defence would ruin everything. So there was a lengthy jockeying for position with pieces marching back and forth as my opponent patiently parried the minor threats.

By eleven the organizers could not conceal their anxiety. The director even ventured to approach our table to inquire of me quietly: 'How long do you reckon the game will last?'

'Don't worry, it won't be long now. At most about three hours.'

He took my reply as a joke. One o'clock, two, three—the guests went home, the spectators too, only the organizers and the other competitors remained. The latter, poor things, had to wait for their earnings in any case. Precisely at three-thirty in the morning, Panno resigned, we got our prizes, and retired to bed. But sleep was impossible. I lay awake until eight, then I took a walk by the sea in the cool of the morning. The prospect held no pleasure for me because as my eyes beheld the first wave it occurred to me that Panno could have achieved a draw if, at the ninetieth move, he had. . . .

Things are much worse when a game is adjourned. Rest is out of the question because the game has to be analysed. The last move is made not on the board but in writing. The record is sealed in an envelope so that the player alone knows it, and he has to foresee his opponent's response. The latter, for his part, is left guessing what may be in the envelope. Apart from unusually clear cases, this means hours of work.

At a tournament in Lima in May 1959, the Chilean master, Letelier, and I were obliged to break off in the middle of an important game. A win would have given me a good chance of first place; a draw would have displaced me. I went straight to my hotel. With dinner out of the question, I ordered lemonade and got down to work. There appeared to be no great difficulty— I was a pawn up in a rook ending. But suddenly I lit on two moves that could be sealed in my opponent's envelope (actually, they were the only likely ones, and would have meant certain defeat for me). By ten o'clock, I knew the game was lost; by eleven I had discovered a surprise defence. That meant starting again from scratch with work on a new plan. All the night through I fluctuated between seeing the game as won and knowing I had no chance. The possible variations grew longer and more numerous. I ordered breakfast in my room and proceeded to classify and check all possibilities. By noon I had decided that, given a correct defence, defeat was certain. Then, after a shower, I set off with a bad headache to play the finish. At two o'clock precisely the judge unsealed the envelope—and at that moment I could have sworn at my friend Letelier, although victory was suddenly within my grasp. He had chosen such a bad move that his defeat was quick and easy. Fifteen hours of hard labour had been wasted—I could have had dinner and gone to the cinema.

When one is in a winning position, work of that kind is bearable, but to adjourn when one is in a weak or losing position is another matter. None of us really wants to accept defeat so we usually seek desperately for a miraculous recovery or, at least, some chance of salvation. It is better to lose at the first sitting than on the second day, because it is easier to go to sleep forgetting the unpleasantness. In the second case sleep is impossible.

Once both I and my opponent spent a sleepless night because we both stood to lose. That was during the 1960 Chess Olympiad in Leipzig. I was playing the Swede, Lundin. Having held the advantage throughout, I ruined my position in a time scramble. Within two hours I had given up hope, but during the night I got out of bed several times, only to convince myself on the chessboard that nothing could be done. On entering the hall next morning, I was resolved to resign forthwith. My opponent was already surveying our interrupted game with a gloomy air. I approached him, meaning to shake hands and sign my capitulation, but he extended his hand first, announcing that he was resigning. The move he had recorded when we broke off was so incredibly weak that he would be mated in a few moves. While I had known all night that I stood to lose, he had known the same about himself, being aware, as I was not, of what lay under the seal. The thought that I might have got in first with my resignation horrified me so much that, ever since, I have always waited to see the other player's move before making my decision.

Adjourned games can be terribly exhausting. To have several in the course of a tournament is a real misfortune. I recall, for instance, an international tournament held in 1949 in the spa town of Trenčianské Teplice in Slovakia. I was in top form and when I met the Hungarian master, Szily, three rounds from the end, I seemed almost certain to win first place. At the adjournment, our game stood as an interesting and highly complicated bishop ending. The night and morning were spent in work, as usual. I discovered some surprising possibilities but my opponent held the trump—with precise defence, he could hold on to a draw. Unwilling to resign myself to this, I searched for other possibilities, but to no avail—again fifteen hours of hard labour. We continued next day for four hours, with Szily playing precisely at first, but then he made a small error which gave me an exemplary victory.

Naturally, I was exhausted. Seeing me pace the spa promenade like a wraith, my next opponent, the grandmaster, Rossolimo, approached me with a friendly offer—since I was obviously tired and a draw with him would give me a first place anyhow, why bother? We could play quickly for a draw, and then go to the cinema.

I would be unlikely to refuse the offer today, but I was twenty-five at the time. Moreover, six months previously Rossolimo had beaten me in Southsea, which had cost me first prize. Now I had to take my revenge! Sacrificing a piece at the outset, I went into a strong attack, only to make a mistake which lost me the game quite quickly.

There was still hope, however. In the last round I met Golombek, against whom I usually won—somehow he suited me as an opponent. To draw with him would have presented no difficulty, but what if Stahlberg were to win against Szily? Then the first prize would escape me!

So against Golombek, too, I sacrificed a piece. In the meantime Stahlberg had scored a draw, but for me a draw was out of the question; it was all or nothing, and as it turned out, it was the latter. I missed first place by half a point.

To this day I curse myself. Had I accepted a draw with Szily, without further play, and drawn the other two games as well . . . or if, having played for a draw with Szily, I had still been half a point short of victory, I would be kicking myself just the same. A chessmaster's life is no joke.

On several occasions in my younger days I muffed things right at the end of a tournament. In Bucharest in 1954 I was greeted with demonstrative acclamation by the public when I defeated my Soviet opponent, Nezhmetdinov—after which, I lost the last three games. On the other hand, at what was my last grandmaster tournament for five years, Athens 1968, I made up for a slow start by winning five games in a row. The difference may be explained by the fact that in Athens I took chess as recreation, my head being full of other matters. Nerves are the number one enemy in the game.

Having used the phrase 'time scramble' more than once, it occurs to me that, perhaps, some explanation is due. When playing a tournament, you have special clocks ticking beside you, something in the nature of double alarm clocks. On making a move, you press the lever on your side, thereby stopping your own half and setting your opponent's in motion, which means that the time he spends in thinking is measured. When at last he has decided his move, it is his turn to press the lever to stop his own clock and start yours.

There is a limit on the time allowed for a given number of moves—usually forty moves in two and a half hours of your time. As the time limit approaches, the clock lifts a little flag, poised infuriatingly ready to drop. If you have completed the forty moves, you can snap your fingers at the flag, but when you have pondered over-long, you may have to get in two, three, or even ten moves with the wretched thing threatening to fall. We call that the time scramble: when the player has to move almost without thought, his eyes on the flag rather than on the board. When both players are pressed for time, the fun really starts. Pieces fly through the air, maybe falling to the ground. Arguments and protests rage.

Time scramble can turn the logical course of a game, or of an entire tournament, on its head. I remember a notable case—in Mar del Plata again, but this was in 1962. In the second half of the tournament I was playing the American master, Donald Byrne. It was one of my best games in the event. Having gained the upper hand, I emerged a pawn up and now I needed to go all out to win. In the middle game I had lost a lot of time, which had landed me in a slight, not critical, time scramble. The flag was up, but my opponent, playing black, was considering his thirty-ninth move so I had only one more to make. Being unfamiliar with the type of clock, I called the referee. As it happened, he was my countryman and good friend Dr. Skalička who, as captain of our team at the 1939 Olympiad in Buenos Aires, had been stranded by the outbreak of war and acquired Argentinian nationality.

'How much longer have I got by this clock, please?' I asked, in accordance with the rules permitting a player to put a question only to the referee.

I was reassured to be told that I had about a minute and a half. Byrne, whose ears were by now pretty red, finally made his move. I made a hasty note of it, spent some thirty seconds in thought, then made a correct counter-move which guaranteed a clear win. Then I made to press the lever—at that very moment the flag dropped, and the rules decree that a move is not complete until the lever has been pressed. Examination of the clock revealed a technical fault—the flag had dropped before the minute hand reached twelve, but according to the rules it is the flag that counts. It is open to the player to check at the start whether the clock is in order, but everyone relies on the organizers.

So I lost the game, to end in seventh place instead of tying for second. Those couple of seconds cost me 650 dollars, a sum which I imagine even the boldest gambler would seldom manage to lose so fast.

Naturally, an opponent's time scramble can be very helpful, but on one occasion I benefited greatly from my own. It happened during the Capablanca Memorial in Havana.

From 1962 to 1967 I visited Havana each year, helping to organize chess and also playing at the annual international tournament. The 1965 event attracted worldwide interest for Bobby Fischer was among the players. Or, to be precise, he was and was not. Offered a special fee, he had accepted the invitation, but then came the problems. American citizens were not allowed to go to Cuba, and no exception was made for Bobby. But the Cubans were not inclined to give in because Fischer's participation was, for them, more than a matter of chess. So they came up with the following idea: Bobby would sit at a chessboard in the Manhattan Chess Club, the club room would be linked by telex with Havana, with a telephone line available as well in case of need. A controller in New York would transmit Bobby's moves to Havana where another controller would make them for him. During transmission the clocks on both sides would stand still, which prolonged play from five to seven hours, and cost the Cubans over 10,000 dollars.

The event was a sensation, though somewhat less so than the events of six or seven years later when Bobby wiped the floor with his three Soviet rivals to become world champion. The papers were full of it all, including some comic interludes. Shortly before the tournament opened, Bobby delivered a public attack on Fidel Castro for, he alleged, trying to turn his participation to political ends. This time Fidel was blameless, his alleged remark having been invented by an American newspaper. So, for a change, I ticked off Bobby in the paper *El Mundo*. Just before starting my game against Fischer, I received an anonymous letter from a Cuban who, evidently, was not much enamoured of Fidel. He wrote: 'During your game with Fischer I shall be in the hall. My eyes will be firmly fixed on you and I am sure you will lose.'

I was really nervous to start with, my attention being focused more on the eyes around me than on the chessboard. Some 5,000 spectators crowded the place every day, however—a number unprecedented at any chess tournament before. Soon I was concentrating on not losing the game. After three or four hours of play, Bobby transmitted his offer of a draw, we exchanged a few words, and I went to refresh myself with a 'Cuba libre', which is Bacardi rum with Coca Cola.

Not long after, I played the Pole, Doda. Anxious to win, I opened sharply, sacrificed a rook for a bishop, and went into attack. But a slight error spoilt it. Doda made an unexpected move, banging the piece triumphantly on the board and then running off to bring any colleagues who happened to be free to see what he had done to me.

Meantime I sat frowning at the board; my ears were certainly dark red. My first impulse was to throw it in and go for several Cuba libres. Then I forced myself to review the situation, which led me to conclude that I was bound to lose. One of the threatened pawns had to go, attack was out. Then I saw a tiny chance—

56

having lost one pawn, I could, with an apparently weak move, offer another. Should my opponent take it, I would sacrifice yet another piece, and he would be in a bad way. Although the course right through to the end was not clear to me, I could see a strong chance of mating. Under normal circumstances it was a faint hope, for my offering the second pawn would arouse my opponent's suspicions and, being no fool, he would see after two moves at least what I already saw. But here was the only alternative to resigning at once.

Finally I hit on an idea for strengthening my chance somewhat. One more check-up confirmed that things stood as I had judged at the start, and now some ten moves remained to me. I had a full hour to make them. Head in hands, I pretended to be seeking a way out, but actually I had decided to put chess out of my mind for most of the hour—I would recite poems to myself or try to recall the logarithms I once knew by heart.

Doda walked the stage as proud as a peacock while other competitors came along to see if my ears were red. Slowly the minutes ticked away; applause greeted the end of someone's game, then quiet again.

With two minutes left on the clock—I had set that as the minimum time for making my ten moves—I reached for a piece to do what I had known for an hour I would have to do. Doda hurried back, then, after brief consideration, he took my pawn. Glancing as if with anxiety at the clock, I made a lightning move, presenting the other pawn. Doda frowned, glanced at my clock, and took the pawn, assuming that, being pressed for time, I had lost control and would offer more pieces. Another swift sacrifice left Doda clutching his head. He thought it over but now it was too late. Even eternity cannot repair the damage of a second, as Zweig wrote. Blow upon blow fell upon the black king, two minutes sufficed for a devastating onslaught. Caught by the time limit, my opponent had to resign. Players gathered round, cursing my luck in having emerged from such a hopeless position, and in a time scramble, too. . . . In this case too big an advantage cost my opponent a whole point in the tournament.

Quiet dramas such as these are enacted at every tournament in every round. Usually the spectators are unaware of them, while to convey after the event what has been going on is hard. Not only is there the theory of the game, requiring thousands of pages to expound even briefly, but also the psychology of chess. It is not enough to know the variants played by an opponent; one must know him as a person too. Character is reflected in style: a timid man will play safe; the dare-devil is capable of the most improbable and possibly quite incorrect combinations.

In its own way, the evolution of chess embodies the evolution of human thought. The polymath and former world champion, Dr. Emanuel Lasker, discovered in his day an interesting parallel between the progress of chess and of military strategy. A. D. Philidor, the leading chess player in the days of the French Revolution, who actually played with Robespierre in the Café de la Régence, discovered the strategy founded on the principle 'the pawns are the soul of the game'. The manner in which he sent these weakest pieces into action was that also employed by the French revolutionary army. Labourdonnais introduced into chess the central breakthrough practised by Napoleon on the battlefields of Europe, while the American Morphy used rapid movements reminiscent of Washington's marches. The Steinitz positional style recalled the trench strategy of the First World War and—here we may supplement Lasker—Alekhine's or Tal's games resemble the rapid mobile actions of the Second World War. True, I am at a loss to show that Bobby Fischer employs the strategy of the nuclear deterrent, but one cannot expect everything to work out precisely.

I have travelled throughout Europe, America and Asia, spending long weeks in all manner of places, sitting endlessly at the chessboard. I have written book upon book about the game, and at times I have worried whether it is not, after all, just a load of nonsense. Think of the mental energy expended on deciding, for instance, whether a pawn should move one or two squares forward, and the amount of paper covered by reflections on these far from earth-shaking problems. Chessmasters squander on these matters the brain power they could well devote to other purposes. I, for instance, might have designed a new type of aeroplane had it not been for such trivia.

Naturally, I have confided these worries to my friends. The writer, Jiří Fried, actually took up the theme in a novel entitled 'Chess Straits'. He rebuts the doubts in the end. A lot of people find pleasure in chess, they enjoy relaxation, entertainment and happy moments, so let the masters rack their brains because they are contributing something towards the ordinary player's enjoyment.

There are diligent players and there are the bohemians. The Hungarian grandmaster, Portisch, is reported to spend eight hours every day studying the game. His time is spent not on writing books or articles, but on preparing ticklish problems for his future adversaries. Grandmaster Pilnik of the Argentine, on the other hand, has never been seen with a chessboard in his home, whereas he was often to be found at a casino or in company elsewhere.

The world of chess embraces those who enjoy the pleasures of life—staying out till the early hours, then sleeping the morning through until play starts in the afternoon—as well as the ascetics. Mikhail Botvinnik, world champion for many years, belonged among the latter. When I visited him in 1960 at his *dacha* near Moscow, he offered me wine, then, recalling that I was due to play that afternoon, he apologized. Accepting a glass none the less, I asked: 'Why don't you have some, Mikhail Moiseyevitch? After all, you're not playing in this tournament.'

He replied that he could not drink because he was preparing for a return match against Tal. This was in June or early July, and the match with Tal was due in March of the following year.

'Forgive me, but if that's how one has to live in order to be world champion, I'd rather not have the honour,' I remarked.

With a smile, Botvinnik poured me another glass of wine, but for himself he took mineral water.

Years ago I thought of writing something in the nature of a travelogue although there was very little I could say about the countries I visited. Most of one's time was spent confined in tournament halls, or with a chessboard in hotel rooms. Free time is devoted to bathing, reading detective stories or playing bridge. Excursions are an unpleasant duty which I have usually avoided because they upset one's concentration.

At times, however, the travelling itself has been exciting. It was not by chance that several of my adventures happened in Yugoslavia because it is certainly one of the most romantic countries in Europe, although the romance is slowly but surely losing the battle with millions of foreign tourists. But in 1960, when I first travelled to a tournament in Sarajevo, things were different. The Bosnian mountains rewarded me with the most interesting episode of my expeditions.

I can still recall every detail. It was Thursday, 31 March, when I set off rather late from Vienna, having overslept that morning. I hoped to cover the 500 miles to Sarajevo in the day. Everything went smoothly as far as the Bosnian town of Banja Luka. I was there by 9 p.m., with only about 140 miles to my destination. A few miles on, however, the trouble started—the road narrowed, the asphalt ended, mighty rocks towered to the right, to the left the ground dropped to the wild mountain river Vrbas. Darkness added to the gloom—not a living soul anywhere. In the end, company appeared in the guise of an enormous lorry racing round a bend in the firm belief that it had the place to itself. Who, after all, would venture to travel this way by night? The only thing was to slam on the brakes. Luckily we both had good ones, and other objects helped to halt us—the lorry's front bumper came up against a verge stone, my back wheel landed in the ditch. Thanks to this, we made no closer contact and our conversation was entirely friendly. While giving me directions for the road, the driver advised me, nevertheless, to spend the night at a near-by inn, the only habitation for miles around.

My zest for work had been aroused, however. My paper had booked a call to Sarajevo for ten o'clock next morning, expecting me to dictate my first dispatch. In any case, I was travelling alone, with no one to dissuade me from carrying on.

Unfortunately, I had misunderstood the lorry driver's instructions. Only when I found myself bouncing in potholes did it dawn on me that I must have been driving for some time along a forest track. Then at the bottom of a steep decline I arrived at the edge of a wood where, in the nick of time, I noticed that the path also ended—before me yawned a big hole, at least four feet deep.

Since there was no question of turning back in the dark, I decided to set out on foot in search of some outpost of civilization. My first steps in the Bosnian mountains ended none too happily, however. My legs slipped from under me in the mud, I rolled down a slope and landed waist-deep in a stream. That sent me hurrying back to the car.

Time passed terribly slowly. With the need to save petrol in mind, I switched on the heating only twice, but after the second time I even managed to doze off. . . . Bow, wow, wow—the most ordinary sound can seem like celestial music. There was I, frozen to the marrow, finding little comfort in the first light of dawn as I peered out at the wild, misty landscape, the sea of mud and the impassable road before me. But where there is a dog, there are people. And sure enough, having waded about a quarter of a mile through the mud, a tiny hamlet sprang up before me, just five or six cottages with smoke starting to rise from two chimneys. The time was about five o'clock, but mountain folk rise early.

On reaching the first cottage, I glanced through the window before knocking. There I saw a solid table and on it—I could hardly believe my eyes—a small chessboard with pieces scattered after an evening game. At that moment I knew I was saved. Chess players are an international fraternity, rather like Freemasons. East or West, in any country you can meet people smitten with the game, and you can always rely on their help when you are in need.

In answer to my knock, a lad of sixteen or seventeen opened the cottage door. His name was Dejibasic Osmo and he was overjoyed when he learnt that a chessmaster from foreign parts had actually turned up in their hamlet. At once he summoned his friend, Mrkena Ejuba, evidently his opponent in innumerable chess matches. Then we set off to review the situation.

It was anything but cheerful. As I had discovered in the night, there was no going forward, and to go back was also impossible. The track had vanished overnight—swept away by the rain. Praise be to you, Dejibasic! You were the first to hit on the truly philosophical thought that if one cannot go back, one must at all costs go forward, be it at the price of a car, or of the established convention that one can drive them only over roads.

So we set out on a truly eventful pilgrimage. The two boys having decided to accompany me, I was surprised when one of them armed himself with a giant axe—the sleepless night must be my excuse for the black thought which passed through my mind. Mrkena's explanation was simple—'We have a lot of wolves and bears around here.' I sweated with delayed fright at the memory of my wanderings the previous night.

We had some twenty miles of cross-country driving to reach the town of Turbe. Having surmounted all obstacles, we arrived somehow by a back way to find we had driven into the Turbe timber yard. We were obliged to ask for the gates to be opened, during which operation a small crowd gathered around my muddy, but heroic Škoda.

At first nobody would believe that we had come from a place where no paths lead and whence, it seemed, only a few army jeeps had made the journey out of sheer necessity at the end of the war. Dejibasic and Mrkena argued fiercely, and after giving their word of honour, called me to witness, brandishing the axe in their excitement. A serious quarrel was brewing, but suddenly, all was clear. Someone in the crowd saw the light, the rest followed, and together they cried: 'Long live Czech machines!'

Later, in reporting my trek, the Yugoslavian papers committed the same error—praising our machines and even the alleged skill of our drivers. To me, however, it was obvious that the credit for this Hannibal-like crossing of the Alps belonged to the two Bosnian lads, and to them alone.

The peculiar atmosphere of chess tournaments is created, in no small measure, by the people taking part. Chess players are of all kinds—the tranquil and the hot-tempered, the quiet and the noisy—but seldom are they bores. Moreover, the same people meet year after year, they visit many different countries together, and usually they become friends. Exceptions are so rare that when two grandmasters turned their contest into a boxing match when playing a tournament in Amsterdam, the episode provided a talking point for many years.

Good chess players are usually people with education and a wide range of interests. The geniuses are different. With Alekhine it was impossible to talk about anything apart from the game. Bobby Fischer, too, always refused any other entertainment or subject of conversation. In Portoroz, once, I called his attention to two pretty girls, asking what he thought of the local beauties. With a contemptuous wave of the hand, he announced: 'Chess is better.'

A crowd of us were in a bar one evening when the bandmaster invited Bobby to sing something. He obliged with zest, naturally earning great applause, which he accepted with a smile. On returning to the table, he told me that Louis Armstrong got 10,000 dollars for a single evening, while he, Bobby, could earn nothing approaching that sum even for an entire tournament. Wouldn't he do better to drop chess and take up singing?

At the time, Bobby was only fifteen, but he was already US champion and held the title of international grandmaster. He went around in jeans and a gaudy pullover, turning up a year later in the same garb at a cocktail party given by our Embassy to celebrate my victory in Mar del Plata. The usual drinks and little savoury delicacies were served. Having stuck it for about an hour, Bobby took his leave of our Ambassador with the words: 'I'm going home, there's nothing to eat here, so I'll go for dinner.'

I had quite a time with him on that South American trip. We encountered each other first in Mar del Plata soon after the start of the tournament when Bobby, full of optimism, told me: 'I have white, and I'll wipe the floor with you.'

I asked if he would allow me to defend myself a bit, to which he replied, with some magnanimity: 'You can do that; at least it will be more interesting.' He went all out, but I happened to be in good form, first playing defensively, then making a counter-attack. On adjournment Bobby was a piece down, but he still hoped for a draw so when he had to resign, he leapt up, swept the pieces to the floor and ran from the hall.

We spent about a fortnight after the tournament in the same hotel in Buenos Aires where we became friends. We even began working together for the next event in Santiago. One day I showed Bobby my secret weapon—a new variation which I planned to use with black in the Sicilian Defence. I had discovered an interesting point involving the sacrifice of pieces. It looked fine and Bobby was unstinting in his praise. In private, however, he found a 'hole' in my analysis; white had a final surprise and it led straight to mate.

Bobby kept his discovery to himself, recording the entire variation in his notebook with the remark: Play against Pachman! In Santiago, however, he drew black, so he was unable to use his weapon. Seldom in my life have I played a game to compare with that against Bobby. We were both leading in the tournament while he had the added incentive of wreaking revenge for his earlier humiliation. He sacrificed a piece, followed immediately by a rook—mate seemed imminent, then, finally, my king escaped across the board to safety. Sweeping his pieces off with an angry gesture, Bobby ran out without waiting to sign his capitulation.

In the next round, I met Sanchez of Colombia. He plays every game 'hard for a draw' and it is no easy matter to win against him. Therefore I was overjoyed when I got him into the Sicilian Defence, actually into the variation for which I had prepared my secret weapon! Naturally, I started to use it, then came a surprise, my king was mated. I eyed my opponent doubtfully—he had revealed himself as a brilliant attacker—when Bobby burst out behind me:

'Sanchez didn't beat you. I upset that variation! He simply played the way I showed him. That's very nice!'

I managed to control myself sufficiently to congratulate Sanchez, and Bobby, too. Without a trace of reproach, I asked Bobby whether it had not occurred to him to tell me about his discovery. He laughed: 'Why should I? I wanted to beat you.'

Some journalists heard this exchange with the result that next day the whole episode was in the press and on the radio. I saw the comic side of the affair because it had obviously not entered Bobby's head that there was anything wrong in his behaviour.

With the help of Sanchez, then, Bobby had caught up with me, but the matter did not end there. Two days later, before the start of play, I was taking a walk with the young Chilean player, Jauregui. We were chatting about this and that, when suddenly on our way to the tournament hall we ran into Bobby.

'Ah, Mr. Pachman,' he called from a distance, 'so today you've been briefing my opponent.'

Realizing at that moment that Bobby was due to play Jauregui, I retorted: 'Of course, Bobby. And I must say he's very well prepared.'

My prompt reply caused Bobby to frown. He pondered the first moves in the ensuing game very deeply. And as it happened Jauregui was using a system I often play, which helped to confirm Bobby's suspicions. He spent one hour and twenty minutes over the first eleven moves, anxious not to play according to the book and so avoid the danger of surprise. In the event, he lost his queen at the twenty-ninth move and was forced to resign at the fortieth. One might almost say that a bad conscience had robbed him of a point, involving the loss of first place in the tournament.

The former world champion was still a boy in those days. Over the years he changed completely. Instead of jeans, he started to wear elegant suits, his prize money went on clothes and soon he was reported to possess twenty-five outfits. His behaviour is, to this day, all his own—the organizers of events never know what to expect of him. In 1967 at the world interzonal championship in Tunisia, he was playing in top form, then he refused to appear for two games, but the loss of these without a fight still left him in the lead. Then he departed, but made an unexpected return to defeat his countryman and rival Reshevsky in a fast game, after which he quit for good. So, by his own doing, he lost his chance for championship title, and in 1972 he was close to repeating the performance, this time at the eleventh hour.

8. Cuba

■.

'Encountering the Young Revolution' was the heading of my first report from Cuba, where I sang the praises of the charming militia girls who guarded my hotel, the Habana Libre—formerly the Habana Hilton. The time was early 1962, shortly after the Bay of Pigs affair. I must admit that I was impressed by the courage with which the Cubans had dared to go their own way so close to the American coast.

On this first visit I made the acquaintance of Fidel Castro. The occasion was a baseball match. Fidel was playing for one of the teams, people yelled at him and when he muffed something they even made fun of him. That delighted me, and it struck me that our President, Antonín Novotný, would never have stood for anything of the kind. We talked afterwards and I discovered that Fidel also played chess. Later I saw him playing a game in which his very second move was a horrible blunder. Apparently members of the Government occasionally held small tournaments among themselves, where Fidel ranked second—I wonder if the others helped him there.

The unchallenged victor in these events was Dr. Guevara, known as 'Ché'. In Europe he would also have been a first-class player. He was a real enthusiast, so much so that during tournaments (from 1962 the annual Capablanca Memorial Tournament was held in Havana) his Ministry can hardly have seen him, because he was always with us, watching nearly all the contests, then playing quick games with us in our free time. Ché was a great but extremely modest man—a true revolutionary and an idealist. I visited him several times in his villa, the last occasion being in September 1964. We were playing chess when he said: '*Sabe, compañero Pachman*, I don't enjoy being a Minister, I

67

would rather play chess like you, or make a revolution in Venezuela.'

Hacer la revolución, that is a typically Spanish, or rather an Iberio-American, expression. Interestingly, he mentioned Venezuela, not Bolivia. That I recall precisely. I also remember my reply: 'Undoubtedly, Commandant, making a revolution is interesting, but one can be more sure of things with chess.'

He laughed, saying that unfortunately he was not as skilled at chess as I was, he had more experience of revolution. Nor did he follow my advice. Six months later he resigned his post as Minister for Industry, left Cuba and made for the mountains of Bolivia. It was not lack of interest in his job, but political differences with Fidel that lay behind his departure, however. It was no secret that Guevara was no lover of the Soviets, preferring Mao as his example. In conversation—in so far as we touched on politics, which rarely happened—he was naturally cautious, but the odd remark now and then left no doubt about his views.

In the summer of 1963 the battle over foreign policy was on. Fidel launched a sharp attack on Soviet policies on the occasion of a big gathering in the Plaza de la Revolución. Euženie was there with me. The four-hour speech was quite a test of endurance, but a slight diversion came around half-time when some bomb or other went off near by. Fidel passed it off with a joke. As people were dispersing around midnight, there were cheers for a group of Chinese—a trade delegation, I think—who beamed with pleasure.

Within a year came the switch. With the economy at sixes and sevens, the Soviets had to pump in millions of dollars daily. Fidel became a realist, Ché went off to die in Bolivia.

From 1962 to 1967 I visited Cuba every year. First I went to help organize chess, then I used to compete regularly in the Capablanca Memorial Tournament. Each time I hoped to find things better, but the trend was precisely the reverse. When the 1966 Chess Olympiad was held in Havana people were living on starvation rations. In the land of coffee, a cup of coffee was a luxury; in the land of tobacco, cigars were strictly rationed. Each year saw a big drive—a record sugar harvest would be the cure for all economic ills. Yet the harvest dwindled relentlessly, not even reaching the level of the Batista days when there was no national mobilization of people to bring it in.

The Olympiad, however, was on a grand scale. Never have I experienced a banquet to match the one held on this occasion. The Government and the Diplomatic Corps were present in full force. And with 300 players in the event, the feast had to be held out of doors. The tables set out in Cathedral Square groaned under the choice dishes—a main course of pheasant, preceded by lobster cocktail. But the onlookers crowding the surrounding houses probably had dry rice for supper—that spoilt our enjoyment.

Fidel summoned me during the evening to ask me to write a book about the Olympiad, to be published in four or five languages. I promised to have a go at it as soon as I got home, but Fidel laughed: 'Oh no, you'll stay right here and write it straight away!'

To gainsay him was difficult, of that I was already aware. Not long before I had been sitting at his table, he offered me a cigar. When I replied that I didn't smoke, he had also laughed, saying, 'If you're a friend of Cuba, try it.' So I tried, I choked, and spent the rest of the evening washing away the taste with Cuba libre.

Now I told Fidel I had to be back in Prague at the latest fifteen days after the close of the Olympiad and one could hardly write a book in that time. He declared it could be done if one went about the job with revolutionary *élan*. Finally we agreed that my countryman, grandmaster Filip, would act as my second in command, and I would have the services of a staff of secretaries, translators and so on.

It was the strangest way of writing a book. I had four big offices and eighteen people at my disposal. Filip and I studied the games played in the Olympiad, then I dictated commentaries in Spanish, and the translators put them into English, Russian, German and French. The system should have worked perfectly, but we ran into all sorts of difficulties. Filip and I had to check all the five languages. We worked twelve hours a day, and at midday and in the evening we plunged numbly into the swimming pool, swam about thirty lengths and then felt a bit better.

In eighteen days the job was done. I still fail to understand how we managed it. Among other things, we had to go through 1,944 games to make a representative selection.

Of course, our record-breaking speed served no purpose—it took six months to publish the Spanish edition, the German appeared a year later, and the others were never printed.

The Olympiad provided two sensations, Bobby Fischer being responsible for the first. The US team was due, by chance, to play the USSR on a Friday, whereupon Bobby demanded that the start be put forward to enable him to finish before sunset, thus avoiding having to play on the Sabbath. The Soviet team refused on the grounds that Petrosian could not start earlier and without lunch. The Americans registered their protest by failing to appear, thereby earning a 0–4 defeat. Of course, the press everywhere was full of the affair. Ultimately, when a replay was held eleven days later, Petrosian took the day off, leaving the Soviet team to score a narrow victory by $2\frac{1}{2}$–$1\frac{1}{2}$ points.

The second sensation was more lasting in nature. It was that the Cuban team got through to the final group A, surpassing the hopes of even the greatest optimists.

When the knock-out round was over that evening, I gave several interviews on the subject for the press and radio, then I retired to my room. Soon a large company burst in. About twenty Cubans, including two Government ministers, sports officials and leaders of the chess federation, had come to celebrate their success with me because, they insisted, as trainer of the Cuban players I had done a lot to bring it about. Their appreciation gave me great pleasure—certainly I could never have guessed that not only would I see Cuba no more than once again, but also that Fidel's papers would refer to me on that occasion as 'a well-known counter-revolutionary'.

9. Journalism and Chess

■▪■▪■▪■▪■▪■▪■▪■▪■▪■▪■▪■▪■▪■▪■▪■▪■▪■▪■

In 1959, apart from my chess activities, I joined the editorial of the daily 'Czechoslovak Sport', later becoming head of its foreign department. My job was not to report or comment on sports events but to devote myself to matters such as the international Olympic movement, problems of amateur and professional sport, and the troubles created by the everlasting 'German question'.

The work of a sports journalist was too simple for my taste, offering little scope for creativity. So I tried now and then to liven things up a bit. During the 1960 Rome Olympics, for instance, I was writing a daily column, but the stuff was as dry as dust. One night I laid a bet with my colleagues that I could invent five sensational items without anyone finding me out. I succeeded, but it could have landed me in trouble. One of my stories told how the famous woman runner, Miss Rudolph, had fallen in love with the no-less-famous runner, Norton—their engagement was soon to be announced. On reading the foreign press in our office, I discovered to my horror that my story had been taken over, first by the Hungarian, Romanian, East German and Polish sports papers, then by 'Soviet Sport' and a Western paper, I think it was the French *L'Equipe*. Things looked bad, because, on her return home from Rome, Miss Rudolph had really got engaged, as if to spite me, to another man. Luckily there was no come-back—perhaps it was difficult by that time to trace the source of this *canard*.

A favourite theme in those days was exposing West German 'imperialism'. In the field of sport we campaigned for East German membership in international sports organizations. Not until 1965–6 did some journalists begin to strike a different note with an attempt to develop something approaching an honest dialogue. The change had come first in literary circles, but by the autumn it occurred to me that a new style might be introduced into sports journalism, too. Munich had just been chosen as the venue of the 1972 Olympic Games, a decision fiercely attacked by all the East European papers.

Recalling the Latin tag, *Audiatur et altera pars*, I went to Munich for a talk with the city's *Oberbürgermeister*, Dr. Vogel. Since my journey had not been approved as a business trip, I had to find the foreign currency myself, but at least the authorities let me have my passport and permission to go. The interview went without a hitch. Its publication marked the first constructive approach to the Munich Olympics in all Eastern Europe.

While in Munich I had the opportunity to inspect the plans for the Games, which led me to an interesting discovery. The Bavarian capital was not, at that date (six years before the event), well off in respect of transport, sports facilities and accommodation—in fact, my impression was that Munich faced very similar problems to ours in Prague. So if Munich could, none the less, act as host why not Prague too?

I visited Munich again early in 1967 for a talk with Willi Daum, Chairman of the German Olympic Committee and of the Organizing Committee for the 1972 Games. We discussed affairs of international sport, including East Germany's status. In the course of our two-hour debate, Herr Daum complained about the intolerance shown by East German clubs and the way they were always bringing politics into sport, while I defended our northern neighbours, retaliating now and then with criticism of the West. In good humour we played back the tape. I declared that it would be passed for publication; Herr Daum laughed heartily, insisting that the story would never appear in our newspapers.

Back in Prague it looked as if Herr Daum had been right. Our chief editor departed immediately on a week's leave, announcing that I could take the consequences. He had had his doubts from the start about my trip, now I would have to consult Party headquarters and the Foreign Ministry. That turned out to be

72

no easy matter although I employed the old trick of telling the Party that the Foreign Ministry agreed to publication, then rushing off to tell the Ministry that the Party had no objection. Actually, objections were raised in both quarters. When the affair had dragged on for several days I got them to agree at least to the interview being published in East Germany if the people there approved.

So I flew to Berlin where I found a strong team awaiting me, composed of sports officials responsible for ideological matters and, of course, a Party man. Their view was unanimous: no question of the interview being published—why, Herr Daum had criticized the GDR! I objected that debate always involves criticism. I, for my part, had stood up for their country so what did they want? Debates of that kind are dangerous, they said, who could tell where they might end. To which I replied that I had put our case so let people judge for themselves. What had we to fear? Evidently the officials were not in favour of letting people judge.

That evening the discussion continued in the more *gemütlich* surroundings of the Budapest Bar. An unexpected arrival was Novoskoltsev, Editor of 'Soviet Sport', who happened to be in Berlin. Without waiting to be seated, he exclaimed: 'Daum?— don't publish!' To my question whether he had read the interview, he replied that he had not, but Daum was an 'imperialist'.

In the end, the wine had a mellowing influence. Although it took us till three in the morning, we agreed that the interview could appear on the condition that an article in the same issue would be devoted to 'unmasking' Herr Daum. When I communicated the news to Prague next morning, they said that I had better write the piece myself, on the spot. To which I objected that I had had my say in Munich, and I had no reason to 'unmask' the gentleman. Further heated discussion resulted in the *exposé* being written by the Germans. It appeared in *Sport-Echo* as an unsigned editorial, but my interview was printed in full, which was undoubtedly the biggest success of my journalistic career up to 1968 (or ever, perhaps). Proudly I dispatched a copy

73

to Herr Daum—in the autumn of 1968 I was able to tell him the whole story.

Following my second trip to Munich, I worked out a project for holding the Olympic Games in Prague. I estimated the overall cost, rather modestly, at 600 million Czechoslovak crowns—three-quarters of which would be highly valuable investment. Certainly it would have been a better undertaking than the pipeline constructed to carry gas from the Soviet Union—it would have cost us much less and would have brought us some return.

I handed the project to various authorities, with an abridged version for the Party leadership. In June 1967, to my surprise, Party approval was given in principle and the Government was instructed to carry out my proposals, which inspired me with bold plans for a motorway, a modern satellite town to serve as the Olympic village, and so on. In short, I was resolved to work full time on the project when the mishap which I describe in the next chapter intervened.

10. A Conflict of Principles

In July 1967 I played at the grandmasters' tournament in Moscow. The event was part of the celebrations on the occasion of the fiftieth anniversary of the Russian Revolution, a circumstance which I was quick to stress in a press interview on my arrival. I said that even if I were to take last place in the tournament, I would hold it an honour and a pleasure to play in celebration of this anniversary. The words were almost prophetic for the start went badly for me, so did the end, and the middle was more or less on the same level. Spassky, Keres and Petrosian wiped the board with me. In the end I was not alone in last place thanks to the fact that grandmasters Filip, Uhlmann and Bilek joined me as companions in misfortune, so the utter disgrace of being in a position where no one is worse off than oneself was, at least, averted.

As usual I spoke at the closing ceremony on behalf of the foreign participants. Naturally, my speech was less about chess and more about revolution, with a few sentences in conclusion devoted to peace, democracy and socialism—all in accordance with the established routine. Greater interest was aroused by a wholly unconventional contribution from Mikhail Tal. Although there was more substance in what he said, my speech was received with applause; during his an embarrassed silence reigned. His actual words were: 'We in the Soviet Union always play at memorial events. First, the commemoration of the famous Chigorin, then of the famous Alekhine, and now we have just finished commemorating—what, I'm not really sure.' Afterwards I learnt that Misha had fortified himself with Dutch courage for that effort.

The newspapers made interesting reading in those days. The Israeli army had struck in three directions, and their Chief Rabbi had uttered these remarkable words: 'Those who don't believe in miracles in this land aren't realists.' Two million Jews against seventy million Arabs—by the laws of mathematics, the outcome could not be in question, for the Arabs were no Bedouins of the last century. They had tanks, planes and rockets even better and more modern than those of the Israelis, and they encircled the tiny country on all sides. There was might behind the declaration by the Palestinian leader, Akhmed Sukeiri, that the Jews would be driven into the sea. The statement was published in our newspapers, and no commentator ventured to add that it belonged to the age of barbarism, nor was there any concern voiced when Egypt concentrated tank divisions in the Sinai Peninsula after enforcing the withdrawal of United Nations units. No one came up with the thought that, according to the definition of aggression proposed by the Soviet Union in the United Nations, the blockade of the Arabian Gulf was in fact an act of aggression. But our press sent up a howl of indignation when the Egyptian tanks met with a crushing defeat. Czechoslovakia was in such haste to break off diplomatic relations with Israel that she even outdid the Soviet Union. The Israelis were dubbed aggressors, militarists, even fascists—all of which struck me as odd, because theirs was the only country in the Middle East where the Communist Party was allowed to exist legally, whereas the Communists in the Arab countries had experienced their St. Bartholomew's Night. I began to have thoughts about the dangers resulting from great-power interests being given precedence over the ideals which I too had extolled in no uncertain terms in the course of my life.

I confided my doubts to several of my Soviet friends. It was quite possible to talk about these matters in private, but when I launched into a debate in the anteroom of the Central Army House in Moscow, even close friends discreetly edged away. Finally, I was so irritated that I sat down in the hotel to write a letter to the Secretary of the Israeli-Czechoslovak Friendship Society in Tel Aviv, Chanan Rozen, whom I had known since

1964. Such heretical ideas could not, of course, be sent through the post so I got Najdorf to mail my letter from America after the tournament ended. Soon it appeared in the paper *Al Hamishmar* —unsigned at the time though my name was published in the same paper a year later.

Back in Prague, I became increasingly annoyed by the constant harping on Israeli aggression in the press. One night—it was 20 June—I could not sleep for thinking about it, so at five in the morning I got up to compose a letter to the Central Committee of the Communist Party of Czechoslovakia.

'Dear Comrades,' I wrote, 'I consider it my moral duty to express my disagreement with the policy pursued by our Republic and the other socialist countries in relation to the Middle East. In my view, this policy is in conflict with the principles of right and justice and therefore also with the true interests of the socialist camp. At the same time I fear that the unobjective propaganda which distorts many of the facts may also have a harmful influence at home by fostering anti-Semitic attitudes among some sections of the population.'

I continued by recalling the assistance rendered by Czechoslovakia to Israel in 1948 when the Arab countries attacked the new state in an undisguised act of aggression. The publicly declared aim of the 'physical destruction of Israel' was, I maintained, a disgrace to any civilized society, while genuine Arab patriots—men like the Chairman of the Communist Party of Lebanon, Comrade Hela—were murdered and persecuted by the reactionary politicians of the United Arab Republic. Support for these policies by the socialist countries was not only contrary to the ideals we proclaimed, it was not even expedient and had dealt a severe blow to our prestige in Africa and throughout the world.

After outlining the policy which I believed to be right, I concluded: 'We advance our views on an issue which arouses concern not only in our country, but in other socialist countries as well, and we believe that our letter will be taken in the spirit in which it is written—as an expression of confidence in the Party, confidence in its endeavour to build a new and happier future here and throughout the world, and to ensure the final victory of the great, humane ideals of Marxism-Leninism.'

At 7.30 a.m. I phoned the writer, Arnošt Lustig, who is known as an expert on Israel. Instead of answering the question I put to him, he exclaimed: 'Hold it, I'm coming over. I must sign it too.' Then, on arrival, Arnošt immediately rang Jan Procházka to ask if we could visit him. Soon we were being offered brandy while Procházka read the letter, declared it was absolutely true and, silencing Arnošt's attempts to explain and debate the matter, saying he had to leave to work on a film, he hastily signed. We departed to deliver our missive to the Party Central Office. I should add that to my signature I appended the title: Chairman of the Communist Party Committee, Olympia Publishing House —that seemed to me correct in correspondence with the Central Committee.

Three days later the Union of Writers met in congress—an event of no special interest to me because authorship of books on chess was no qualification for membership of that body. However, when Arnošt phoned me that evening, I could tell from his voice that something had happened. He informed me that our letter had come under strong attack from Hendrych, head of the Central Committee delegation, when addressing a meeting of Communists attending the Congress. He had cited it as an example of incorrect views among intellectuals. But instead of applause, or cries of 'Shame!', people had shouted that they wanted to hear the letter to which he was referring. Hendrych responded by announcing that he had not got it with him, whereupon Arnošt rose to say he had a copy and would read it out. When he finished, the applause came. Ladislav Mňačko announced that he would like to add his signature; Pavel Kohout said the same, and others followed them. Whether the historic debate on Israel which initiated the atmosphere of criticism and dissent at the Writers' Congress would have happened without this episode is difficult to say—probably it would have developed in any case, but the fact remains that Hendrych's ineptitude was responsible for sparking it off.

During the following days we learnt more about events at the Congress. Ludvík Vaculík's speech, with the key passage about 'a regime which has not managed in twenty years to solve a single human problem', started circulating in Prague. At first I was somewhat taken aback by the statement, but then I had to admit that there was some truth in it and that there really was room for improvement in this socialism of ours. By the time our Party committee met I was able to talk as if I had actually been present at the Congress. On the whole our members were in favour, although some said that perhaps these intellectuals were going a bit far.

A few days later I was invited to present myself at the Party headquarters where I was reminded that the Middle East was a highly sensitive area in the conflict with imperialism and my friends and I were, by our attitude, playing into the hands of the imperialists; we should keep quiet and do a bit more thinking. The latter I promised to do, but about keeping quiet I made no comment. Further thought failed to convince me that it was my duty to do so. True, that may have been because I could devote only a few days to the subject before departing for Cuba to play in the Capablanca Tournament.

On returning to Prague at the end of September I learnt that I no longer held the post of Foreign Editor of our paper. Apparently it had been decided that I should confine myself to writing about chess. Since the reasons were obvious, I merely inquired if the decision was the Chief Editor's. No, I was told, it had come from 'higher quarters'.

Writing about chess seemed to be an inadequate reason for remaining on the staff—I could write at home in peace and quiet. A special Party conference was called to consider the situation and the question of my chairmanship of the branch. The committee members were present to a man, plus the director of the publishing house, our former Chief Editor, his successor, and representatives of Central Office. My former chief, who had once assured me in the intimacy of my home: 'Luděk, you're my only friend. Without you, I'd feel like an alien in Prague,' now tried to catch me out by asking whether the recent aggressive acts perpetrated by the Israeli Zionists had not caused me to change my mind. I replied that, on the contrary, they had confirmed my view because the last Communist party in the Arab world had just been banned—in the Sudan, if I remember rightly. In my simple way I saw the banning of a Communist party as a sin against democracy. Again I explained my reasons for objecting to Israel being labelled as the aggressor in the current conflict, and I spoke in favour of our renewing diplomatic relations.

The outcome was that I would be given six months' unpaid leave, after which I would terminate my employment.

Towards the end of September I had an unexpected visit from František Vodsloň, subsequently to become known as one of the 'men of January' [January 1968, which started the 'Prague Spring'—translator's note]. A Communist from the age of seventeen, Vodsloň had been condemned to death by the Nazis but by some miracle the sentence was changed to life imprisonment. After the war he had held governmental posts and been a member of the Party Central Committee. As early as 1956 he had voiced views similar to those which spread and took deeper root after January 1968, and this had caused his transfer to the post of chairman of the physical training organization—a convenient dumping ground for uncomfortable characters. Vodsloň was not happy there because he was interested in politics not sport. By the spring of 1967 he had been relegated to a humbler position in the organization, but he was still a member of the Central Committee, which was his reason for coming to see me. On the agenda of the next meeting was a motion to expel from the Party four leading writers—Ludvík Vaculík, Pavel Kohout, Ivan Klíma and A. J. Liehm. This worried Vodsloň, who told me that Vaculík's speech to the Writers' Congress struck him not as an attack on socialism but as something to which he too would be ready to put his name. Believing me to be a bit of an expert on matters concerning intellectuals (which I was not), he had come in search of information. He took his task so seriously that he was hastily reading books by all four rebels. On talking things over, we found ourselves in full agreement—instead of expelling the writers, the Party ought, we felt, to give serious consideration to the criticisms voiced at their Congress. And, at the Central Committee meeting, František spoke out in their defence and was among the five who voted against expulsion.

11. The Prague Spring

On 3 January 1968 I attended a big reception at the Cuban Embassy in Prague. I was flattered to be told that my article about Ché Guevara was, so they said, 'the only good article about him to appear in Czechoslovakia'. To this day I have a great respect for Dr. Guevara, a true revolutionary idealist, a man who saw revolution as the means of liberating his fellow men and for whom the offices and the honours it brought in its wake were unpleasant duties.

At the reception I talked with many acquaintances—primarily diplomats whom I had met at our embassies in various countries. The topic of the day was the meeting of our Party's Central Committee, then in session. It was already common knowledge that Antonín Novotný's throne was tottering. Would the President-cum-Party Leader survive nevertheless, or could we expect a big shake-up in our domestic affairs? Most people I spoke to believed that no great change would come—Novotný might be replaced in due course, but policies would continue as before.

Later in the evening news spread among the company that Alexander Dubček had been elected First Secretary of the Party in place of Novotný. For those without inside knowledge of Central Committee affairs he was rather an unknown quantity. We knew that he had studied in Moscow and had recently clashed with Novotný over the Slovak question, the issue which had triggered off this momentous session. The view that evening was that, on the whole, any change must be for the better.

About a week later, the Party committee at the Olympia publishing house came up for re-election, but since the wind of change had not yet affected Party work to any noticeable extent, the decision that I was to resign the chairmanship still applied. I prepared to settle down to work at home, when unexpectedly I received an invitation to lecture on chess at the University of Puerto Rico and to give some training to chess players. The salary was attractive and would help towards the holiday we planned to have in Italy. I hesitated, nevertheless. It looked as if things would be lively in Czechoslovakia in the immediate future. So I suggested to the new chairman of our branch that we call a meeting to hear a report on the Central Committee proceedings in December and January. We would invite Vodsloň or another member who had taken an active part in the defenestration of Novotný or, failing that, I would like to speak myself. But the new committee was none too keen on the idea; it would be better to wait for instructions from the top. This attitude depressed me so much that it speeded my departure. If people were still sitting tight waiting for orders, probably nothing new was to be expected. At the beginning of February I left for San Juan.

Puerto Rico seemed, in its natural features, like a smaller version of Cuba, and, with its towns, streets and bars, like a shot from an American Western. Soon I was busy giving chess courses for beginners and advanced students, and meeting eight or nine of the best Puerto Rican players. In an exhibition game against the young, talented international master, Caplan, I narrowly escaped losing my authority as a teacher. I saved myself at the eleventh hour with a draw. The days passed rather monotonously and the heat was exhausting. Despite the kindness of my hosts and their enthusiasm for chess, I soon regretted having accepted the invitation. The trouble was that I could tune in to Prague radio, and the more I listened, the more I was amazed. It was like a thriller, and as a journalist I was keenly aware of how many events had been packed into those few weeks.

In March, Novotný was given the sack for the second time—from the office of President—and he was succeeded by Ludvík Svoboda, whom I had known in the days when he was Chairman of the Office for Physical Training and Sport. So now I wrote my congratulations, also taking the opportunity to do a bit of propaganda for my Prague Olympics idea. I hoped to work hard on it when I got home, as the sins of 1967 would surely be forgotten—even the expelled writers were back in the Party. My one wish was to be home but my contract required that I stay until May. Listening to the broadcast of the May Day celebrations, I was quite moved. Even at that distance you could tell how different it all was to the days when we used to shout about the red flag of socialism flying over lands stretching from our western borders to Shanghai. I was sad not to be marching with the others.

Naturally, not everything I observed from abroad seemed good. I wrote two critical articles for papers back home, but that was the sum total of my political output between January and June 1968—I was fully occupied with chess tournaments. What, then, was my surprise when at a later date the Prosecutor maintained that 'the defendant was among the active initiators of the so-called revival process'. That was, indeed, undeserved praise.

My arrival in Prague coincided with Victory Day, 9 May. The place was full of excitement, but—contrary to my usual habit—I had no desire to raise my voice. To my mind there was too much talk; action was needed—some cleaning up at Party headquarters and in other high places, for instance. Of course, I was delighted at the freedom of speech and the way the press had woken like a sleeping beauty from its long slumbering. Now one could have had a real dialogue with Herr Daum!

Following the Czechoslovak championship in Luhačovice, where I came to grief, taking fifth place for the first time in all the years I had competed in this contest, I took part in a tournament in the West German town of Solingen. Patron of the event was the then Minister of Justice, later Federal President, Heinemann. I got into discussion with him about world affairs, and about Czechoslovakia in particular. He told me that they fully sympathized with our democratic aims but anything other than moral support would lay them open to accusations of interfering. I replied that moral support is excellent, but a little interference —for instance, a nice round sum of 500 million dollars—would also be in place. A loan of this amount was being widely discussed at the time. Herr Heinemann laughed at this, saying that chess players evidently take a very practical view.

The moving spirit at the tournament was Herr Evertz, chairman of the local club. I was told that he was financing the event. He was wealthy but was counted among the enlightened capitalists, being far from tight-fisted. He struck me as very young, and he had started, it seemed, as an ordinary worker, then worked his way up thanks to an invention he made. From which it is evident that capital is not necessarily gained by robbery, as Marx maintained.

I read in the German papers about the publication in Prague of a manifesto entitled '2000 Words', signed by many well-known people and composed by Ludvík Vaculík. It seemed to have met with disapproval from the Party leaders and the Government. A reporter from the local Solingen paper asked me to comment, which I did, since the extracts from the manifesto which I had read in the press seemed quite reasonable and Vaculík had made a great impression on me with his speech to the Writers' Congress. The interview appeared under the militant caption, 'We'll take to the barricades if we must.' That was not my idea but I felt that it chimed with the needs of the day. In theory we had two alternatives. The first called for extreme caution: while quietly throwing out the hardliners and bullies from their cosy nooks, we would have to soothe the Soviets by insisting that nothing was really happening. Then, after holding the Party congress and a general election, the flood-gates could be opened to everything which made the spring of 1968 so wonderfully exciting—freedom of the press, freedom of assembly, and all those areas of freedom which seem so commonplace except when they're prohibited. Now, however, it was too late to take that course. There remained the second—openly and with all speed convene the congress and hold the election in a matter of weeks. Naturally, the possibility of Soviet military intervention had to be reckoned with and we should have to prepare for it by partial mobilization and manning of the eastern frontiers, accompanied by a proclamation to the world that we would defend our territory against all comers. Far be it from me to suggest that we could have won a war against the USSR. War was the last thing I could have wished, but I was convinced that a public declaration of our intent to resist would discourage plans for military action.

Today I am even more firmly convinced of that. Early in 1969 a member of a delegation to Moscow from a 'fraternal Communist Party' told me that the final decision to intervene in Czechoslovakia was made as late as the night of 17 August 1968. Nine members of the Soviet *Politburo* were present when the vote was taken, Kosygin, Shelepin and Mazurov voted against invasion, that old fox, Suslov, abstained, while five were in favour. So five out of nine! What, I wonder, would have been the result if our troops had been manning the frontier? The hotheads like Shelest would have found it much more difficult to get a majority. Moreover, I think now, as I did in June 1968, that a nation cannot allow itself to be crushed repeatedly—the effect on its character, its psyche, is far from healthy.

I found on my return from Solingen that people were worried about the disinclination of the Soviet troops to withdraw from our territory after completing manoeuvres. I too felt that no guest should outstay his welcome, so I wrote an article for the railwaymen's paper in which I used some interesting information from the Ministry of Transport to refute the argument that transport problems were delaying the troop movements. The matter still worried me, however, and one sleepless night I penned a letter to the Soviet Embassy. 'Dear Comrades,' I wrote, 'I address you in the name of the deep friendship which has existed between our countries for over twenty years and which our people have regarded as the backbone of our policies, the guarantee of our national being.' Having pointed to the damage to our mutual relations resulting from military interference in our domestic affairs and to the genuinely socialist nature of the changes in our country, I declared that under no circumstances would we allow anyone to destroy our hope for the future. 'Many times in the past our people have proved their loyalty to friends. They also proved, however, five centuries ago, that they can stand firmly by their ideals.'

Today I would put many things differently. I would not, for

instance, make the sweeping assertion at the beginning about what people thought of our policies because each must realize that for himself. The Ambassador must also have found my threats about 'five centuries ago' rather ridiculous. I was referring to the brave followers of John Hus whose glorious victories were followed, of course, by the White Mountain (the battle in 1620 which brought Bohemia under Hapsburg rule), when our national honour was salvaged in part by a mere thousand Moravians fighting with their backs to the wall against terrible odds. Undoubtedly the White Mountain broke something in us; since that day we have definitely not been addicted to experiments in taking on all comers. This was demonstrated in 1938. In June or July 1968, *Der Spiegel* was already prophesying that, in the event of Soviet military intervention, armed resistance was not to be expected from Czechoslovakia. Yet one cannot be wise before the event. The enthusiasm of that spring was such that the Hussite spirit might easily have awoken within us, and I was not to know that it would not.

Shortly after writing the letter, we left for our holiday in Italy. The trip was in the nature of a present to my mother-in-law on her sixty-fifth birthday. It was our best holiday of all time. We arrived home on 16 August.

12. Seven Days in August 1968

▪▪▪▪▪▪▪▪▪▪▪▪▪▪▪▪▪▪▪▪▪▪▪▪▪▪▪▪▪▪▪▪▪▪▪▪▪▪▪

I was half asleep, disturbed by strange sounds, when the telephone rang. I recognized the voice of Dana, Emil Zátopek's wife: 'Luděk, the Soviets are occupying us!'

At first I thought it was a stupid joke—Dana was fond of joking and she had called more than once at odd times; but now the sounds were growing louder. I realized she was serious, so I sat up in bed, and looking at my watch, I saw it was exactly half past one. The thing was strangely unreal. It is easy to say, 'The Soviets are occupying us,' but can it really happen, simply occupying a country? For years I had spoken and written about our allies and friends, and I even believed what I wrote. Can one's friends steal in by night?

I turned on the radio. A statement by the Party leadership and the Government was being relayed. The occupation had taken place without the consent of the Party or the Government; neither the armed forces nor the public were to offer any resistance. Calls for calm and discipline. And still it all seemed unreal.

I phoned several friends. Dana told me that shortly before she first rang me, Emil had been called to duty at the Ministry of Defence. Others knew no more than I did. Should I go somewhere, do something? But where, and what could one do?

Around seven I could stand it no longer, so I went into the city centre. Quite aimlessly I made for the scene of the main drama in May 1945—the radio building. An improvised barricade was being erected, an overturned tramcar, a Russian-made automobile, some paving stones. I wandered around for a few minutes, then a squad with submachine-guns drove us away. The first tanks appeared in the street.

As I walked down Wenceslas Square, shots sounded behind

88

me. Did that mean there was fighting? On reaching the office of the Party daily, *Rudé právo*, where the paper I had worked on also had its office, I went in. Perhaps I would get some news there, I might even be able to do something. My former colleagues welcomed me, but they knew nothing. The radio was still broadcasting. At about nine o'clock, someone rushed in shouting that we must all clear out, the Russians were occupying the building. Unwilling to obey, I stayed with two of the editorial staff and a secretary. Soon troops arrived; their officer addressed us in Russian:

'If you please, you are ordered to leave.'

I replied quite illogically that I took orders from no one but the First Secretary *Tovarysh* Dubček. It was illogical, because I had never in my life received an order from Dubček, and it was highly unlikely that he would ever give me one. The officer pondered my reply, then he told me not to cause difficulties. To which I retorted that the occupation was illegal, but he said he had his orders. He beckoned to two men armed with tommy-guns, who lifted me from my chair and conducted me downstairs. On the way I heard an exchange between the officer and the secretary, who, incidentally, had always been an entirely unpolitical person:

'Please, there's a good girl!'

'I'm not going anywhere, I belong here.'

'Be a good girl, I beg of you.'

'I won't move, and that's that!'

They literally carried her out of the building.

Some of us held an informal conference in the street. Obviously all editorial offices and printing shops would be occupied, but perhaps our administrative office, which was in another street, would be free. We would try that, and then we must find a small printing press, because the paper ought to come out and say something—what, was not yet clear. Should we call for calm, or arouse people to action?

We managed to find a small duplicating firm where we could, at least, produce a makeshift 20,000 copies. Three of us went to arrange the details. Naturally, we were anxious to work secretly since we expected a clamp-down by the occupying power at any moment. We would probably have to go underground, to sleep away from home, to cut ourselves off from families and friends.

Unforeseen problems arose at the printer's. For instance, we needed only one of the seven women employees for our job, the others were to stay home to avoid danger. Who would volunteer? With one voice, all seven came forward, and not one would back down. They brushed aside the question of who had or had not got a family. Were they to be punished for having children? Finally it was agreed they would take turns.

Not a word was said about my not being on the staff, everyone accepted me. When I managed to contact some Party officials whose attitude was in no doubt, I learnt that next day a press commission would be meeting; it would be composed of people from the press, radio and television and its job would be to handle information on the political situation, co-ordinating the work of the various media. I was invited to join on behalf of the two sports papers, *Československý Sport* and *Stadion*, thereby, in effect, assuming the political direction of both.

Most of the editorial and administrative staff of our paper worked with a will. But the chief editor absented himself by continuing his holiday some fifty miles from Prague, undoubtedly congratulating himself on his wisdom—he could avoid committing himself to one side or the other, then, when things settled down, he could return to soldier on under whatever régime had come out on top. But in any event this success was short-lived: he was dismissed from the editorship in 1970 on the grounds that, in August 1968, he had not returned to Prague in order to stop the goings-on of Pachman and company. How he was supposed to have accomplished that, poor fellow, is a mystery to me and, I imagine, to him as well.

We divided our editorial team into three groups—the first worked in our emergency offices, the second stayed in hiding with friends, ready to take over should the first group be arrested, while the third roamed the streets to pick up news items. There was plenty of excitement. During the first few days, for instance, people were arguing with the Soviet troops, firmly refuting the various 'reasons' for their entering our country. Emil Zátopek dominated the scene in Wenceslas Square on the first evening. I was with him, watching as he literally hurled himself at groups of soldiers, introducing himself by name plus all his sports titles, then adding an invitation in Russian, 'Now let's talk!' At once, a crowd would gather and there would be an impromptu meeting.

Within a couple of days the first contingents were so badly infected by our arguments that thousands had to be withdrawn from the city. The fresh units evidently had orders not to talk and, in any case, interest was waning on our side because Russian photographers had been busy around the debaters, enabling the Soviet press to carry 'evidence' of how our people were fraternizing with their troops. So we issued an instruction by press and radio that the campaign of persuasion should stop— within an hour not a soul was to be seen near the Soviet soldiers.

News was coming in all the time—about the Party Congress held on 22 August in a big Prague factory right under the noses of the occupying forces, about the response abroad to the events in our country, the debate in the United Nations, and so on. We received full information about the situation as far as our armed forces were concerned. As far as I remember, it was on 23 August that a real outburst threatened: a tank brigade, in virtual defiance of its officers, set out to have a go at the Russians. A delegation rushed from Prague to beg and persuade the men to desist, and finally the danger of a clash was averted. News came, too, about the first victims of 'fraternal aid'. A nineteen-year-old girl was shot dead while distributing leaflets, two lads in a lorry were shot by a patrol—they must have failed to notice the order to halt. No more discussion, it was simpler to show that might is right.

All these matters were discussed in the press commission, jobs were shared out and we returned to our offices. I always called a brief editorial meeting to report what I had learnt. There were no secrets among us, and I believe that never in history can a political leadership have had such implicit confidence in the press as in those days. We were, in effect, given a free hand to decide what to publish and what to keep for our own information.

There were technical difficulties with distribution. Troops holding the bridges over the river Vltava stopped and searched all cars. But various ways were devised for overcoming this obstacle. For instance, a fleet of fishing boats would appear on the river—the Prague Anglers' Club was having a field day. Hidden under the bridge on one bank was a car from which papers were loaded into a boat; on the other side they were transferred again to the car which had, in the meantime, passed the check-point above.

We lived in daily expectation of stern reprisals. The rumour went round, for instance, that the signatories of the '2000 Words' manifesto were due for arrest at any moment. Realizing that I had not been among the tens of thousands who had signed, I hastened to give the following statement to the press:

TO THE OCCUPYING FORCES

You are arresting, or you intend within the next few hours to arrest, the signatories of the '2000 Words'. Having been abroad for some time, I have not yet signed the document. Therefore I append my signature today. My respects, your former friend,

Luděk Pachman

Was there any value in the gesture? In my opinion there was; I felt we needed to boost public morale.

I wrote brief editorials for our paper and one longer article on collaboration. Under the heading, 'The Hour of Truth', it concluded as follows: 'Allowing that some people place their careers above the fundamental values which are the stuff of life—honour, right, decency—let them nevertheless bear one thing in mind: namely, that invaders come and go. As civilization advances, the speed of their departure is apt to be accelerated. The first occupation of our country lasted three hundred years, the second a mere six, and we are all convinced that the time curve will, in the present case too, sink by geometrical progession. Invaders come and go, but the nation, the people remain. And the people do not forget!'

The article was already printed when it struck me that some of the high-flown phrases were cribbed, taken indeed from a most unsuitable source! Stalin it was who said: 'Hitlers come and go, but the German nation remains.' What a blunder! People would think I was still in the grip of Stalinism! Seizing a copy from the press, I rushed off to our headquarters where a Party meeting was in progress. On the way I ran into an incident in which Soviet troops were shooting at the windows of a building. People in the street tried to hold me back, but I insisted that I must get to an urgent meeting. Actually it was not so vital, but in those days we felt that every job must be done, even if it was of no real use.

Altogether, as time was to show, the public proved themselves to be better than their leaders. They tried their utmost to do something. Young people demonstrated in Wenceslas Square, workplaces were on the alert for calls to action, lightning strikes always won an enthusiastic, unanimous response.

Power rested, in effect, with the press, radio and television, because everyone followed their lead. For instance, in response to a broadcast suggesting how to hamper foreign agents reported to be armed with lists of people to be arrested, the nameplates of streets and the numbers on houses vanished within two hours.

The streets were plastered with slogans, one of the most popular being: 'Lenin wake up, Brezhnev's gone mad!' Brand-new songs were to be heard, such as the famous 'Ivan go home, Natasha's waiting for you', and the Russian revolutionary song 'Partisan' was given new words—the last verse went as follows:

> Brezhnev's pulled the plug
> on friendship for all time.
> Kosygin's hopping mad.
> Lenin, into battle!

It was probably the biggest upsurge of popular creativity in all time. The Dutch chess grandmaster, Donner, who was in Prague at the time, roamed the streets exultantly proclaiming: 'This is a battle of paper against tanks, and it's not even certain that the paper will lose!'

I asked if he would like to appear on television. He agreed at once, so we set off for the new suburb where the emergency studios were located on the top floor of an unfinished building. We had been given precise instructions about how to proceed. Only two people at a time were to cross the building site; they were to behave unobtrusively, not look round and keep their mouths shut. On my first visit, I had not been able to resist following the example of Lot's wife, and the sight was worth it— the balconies of the house opposite were crowded with people staring, pointing and gesticulating. Obviously they all knew about the television studios.

On the third day of occupation, a radio announcement said that Emil Zátopek was in danger, he must go into hiding. But one of our staff told me next morning that Emil was walking about town, easily recognizable under a Sherlock Holmes cap. We sent two of our people to detain him, with instructions to get help from the police if necessary. They caught him in the act of pasting up an enormous poster on a corner of Wenceslas Square, quite oblivious of the presence of a Russian soldier a few feet away. The soldier approached, stuck a gun into Emil's back and looked threatening. Emil turned round with a laugh, held out his hand and said in Russian: 'That's O.K. *tovarysh*,' after which he retreated round the corner to put up another poster.

Soon I was giving him a good scolding. 'But it's so sad in hiding,' was his reply. So I put him in the car to take him across the river to the television place. I instructed him to keep quiet during the check-up on the bridge and let me do the talking.

When the guard stopped us, I jumped out with alacrity, saying: 'Do you want me to open the boot?' He melted completely at this willingness, but at that moment Emil leapt out, declaring with much gesticulation: 'Even a dog wouldn't stand for what you've done to us!' The guards, two of them, moved ominously towards him, but I stepped between them, explaining politely that my friend had had a drop too much—they would know how it was, we had celebrated a birthday and he didn't know when to stop. For this they showed great understanding and accepted my promise to take him straight home. After that, Emil was very meek, assuring me it would not happen again.

I was sleeping in a different place each night, although one could hardly speak of sleep. For the sake of secrecy, I used two cars—in short, I felt like a spy of the first order. The papers came out; people literally tore them from our hands at the factory gates; railwaymen carried them out of Prague. Once a police car stopped us in the street. The officers asked if they could help, otherwise they had nothing to do, so we gave them a thousand copies and allotted them a beat.

On 26 August, in the afternoon, we learnt that an 'agreement' would probably be signed in Moscow, and it boded ill for us. The public knew nothing as yet—they were still painting slogans and demonstrating—but we were filled with gloom. Had it all been in vain? Was a new Munich on the horizon? Early next morning I went to the television centre. The building site was deserted, the rooms empty, cameras and tape-recorders lay scattered around—a paradise for thieves, but, remarkably, there was no stealing in those days—the Prague underworld must have gone on strike. I was horrified, had everyone given up and was I battling on alone?

But within half an hour, people arrived. No one knew what to do. Naturally, it would have been simple to announce that the agreement was unacceptable, that passive resistance should continue. But Dubček and Svoboda, whose names were chalked up on every street corner, had evidently signed the document. Could we come out against them? People would not know whom to believe. The best thing was to go to the office, prepare the issue and wait for news. That, when it came, was as bad as I had expected.

At midday—with perfect timing—our Chief Editor arrived back from his holiday. We called a staff meeting, at which I made a farewell speech. I felt a bit like crying, but a young journalist and a typist did it for me—I must have piled on the agony too much. Then we all went for lunch before saying good-bye. Everything was so unreal, and I was terribly tired.

I met my wife, and we walked down Wenceslas Square, still full of people. By the statue an impromptu meeting was in progress. Someone was speaking into a loud-hailer about national pride and the need to stand firm. Unable to resist, I clambered on to the plinth and, wandering somewhat from the point at issue, I talked about the Hussites and the Orphans [the name given after the death of the Hussite commander, Žižka, to his followers; following a split in the Hussite ranks, the Orphans were defeated in 1434 at the fratricidal Battle of Lipany—translator's note]. Then I recalled what happened after the Battle of Lipany, and how really things always seem to turn out badly like that. When I had climbed down, a girl student embraced me, and a foreign reporter dragged me to his room in the Yalta Hotel. He was from Norwegian television and was overjoyed to find I was a chess grandmaster. Standing me with my back to the window in order to have a backdrop of Wenceslas Square, he started firing questions. I have no idea what I said, but I remember wondering what the Norwegians would do with it, and altogether what could be done. My doubts were justified, because soon nobody was doing anything about it. After a burst of indignation the world fell silent.

The Norwegian handed me on to his colleagues. I believe that was when I first met Dick Verkijk of Dutch Radio, whom I was to meet again on other occasions, as I shall recount later.

That afternoon I was at home for the first time in seven days. First I had a long bath, then I gazed into space, after which I started writing. In the evening I drove into town with two or three articles about the August events, something in the nature of a proclamation, and a letter to the International Chess Federation. I hoped to find a foreign journalist to take the letter out of the country for me, but I never reached the hotel. Near the city centre I saw a young man desperately waving a crutch. When I stopped, he said: 'Please could you drive me home? The trams aren't running and I could never get there on foot.'

With difficulty I helped him into the car. Both his legs were paralysed. At first he was silent, then he burst out: 'It's terrible—we can't all just pack it in!'

I made no reply, but he went on to ask what I thought. So I told him that probably everybody had packed it in. Perhaps this was the end, or it might just be the beginning—who could tell?

96

'We've decided we won't give up, we'll go on fighting.'

When I asked about the 'we', he replied that they were a group of young people who had been distributing newspapers by the National Museum and had organized the collection of signatures to a statement condemning the occupation and demanding neutrality for Czechoslovakia. As we entered a square where the lights were bright, he looked at me: 'Haven't I seen you recently on television?'

I said it was possible and, at his request, told him my name. As he got painfully out of the car, he bent towards me, whispering: 'If we need anything, can we ask you to help us?'

When I said yes, he added in an even lower voice: 'Then we'll call you. The password will be Johann Hus.'

He hobbled away, to disappear in a doorway. I sat for a while in the car, thinking.

13. A Turbulent Autumn

■.

Those first days after August were like a dream. I spent most of my time at the typewriter, composing various tracts. I sent letters to sundry statesmen—the first going to Kadar in Hungary because he was reputed to be a chess player. Surprisingly, it received quite a lot of publicity. Here are two paragraphs:

'On 21 August, it was clear at a stroke that the matter at issue was not one of a few reforms, but of a relentless struggle against a sham which went under the name of socialism in order to mask its true aims, its egoistic great-power interests and its Tsarist mentality. . . .

'You should be aware that even after 21 August there are people among us who have not lost faith in socialism and who want to strive for genuine socialism. For that very reason we are labelled as counter-revolutionaries. . . .'

I learnt later that Kadar read the letter, and he was not particularly annoyed—probably he knew how things were and had his own ideas about them.

To several papers, including the Polish *Trybuna ludu* and the East German *Freie Welt*, I sent replies to their accusations of Zionism, counter-revolution and other sins. I also duplicated a statement to friends in all the five Warsaw Pact countries, in which, having told them off about the invasion, I added in conclusion, 'Decent people of the world, unite!' For *Der Spiegel* I prepared a long article on the August events, but by some mistake it came into the hands of a journalist from one of the sensational rags, who made an incredible hash of it. After that, for some obscure reason I wrote what purported to be a personal confession, under the heading, 'The Birth of a Counter-Revolution'. It was published in the West German *Christ und Welt*

98

which, in view of what was to follow, was highly symbolic. The conclusion really went a bit too far, though some people liked it—an indication of their bad taste or mine, or perhaps both. Euženie protested strongly, saying they would certainly put me in prison for it. In a way, she was right—they did put me in prison, but not on account of that article.

In mid-September I went abroad since, by virtue of my profession, I still held a passport with exit permits for all countries. I gave as the reason for my trip that I had to find a publisher for my books on chess. Hitherto the German editions had been published by the East German *Sportsverlag* with whom, in the heat of the August events, I had cut off all relations, although they had done me no wrong and the order to invade Czechoslovakia had not come from them. But in any case they would have thrown me out following the argument with *Freie Welt*.

I had no definite plans, but it occurred to me that I might drop in on my friends in West Germany. It is, after all, the biggest European country and if anything could be done, it was there. The short-wave transmitter *Deutsche Welle* offered an excellent medium for having a go at the Soviets.

In Munich I tried to carry out an undertaking I had made to our chess organization. Our most talented young master, Luboš Kaválek, had left Czechoslovakia soon after August. I might almost say he was my pupil—at least that was his contention. In any case we were friends and I was upset that he had not told me of his decision. Probably he was afraid I would object, although he had a strong reason to leave since his father, who had emigrated in 1948, was employed as a music editor with Radio Free Europe. Kaválek's loss was a serious blow to our chess forces, and I had been detailed to have a talk with him. My efforts to persuade Luboš to return were fruitless, but we did agree to register a protest by refusing to take part in the Chess Olympiad due to be held in Lugano. We would issue a joint statement and try to get FIDE, the International Chess Federation, to go on record as condemning the uninvited entry of troops into our country as an infringement of its principles. We planned to be in Lugano for the start of the Olympiad.

On my return to Prague, I phoned Jan Procházka. We agreed to invite a few writers and two of the 'men of January' to meet in my flat for a discussion about what to do. There were about twelve of us, and as many opinions as people present. A young writer came up with the fantastic idea that one might kidnap the Soviet Politburo representative, Kuznetsov, or shut him up in the Writers' Union house at Dobříš near Prague. We would force him to sign a 'Dobříš Protocol' as a parody of the 'Moscow Protocol' signed by our leaders in August. It would be an international joke, and humour is, he maintained, the prime weapon of the Czech nation. We had to reject the plan, however, because we were faced with the problem that Comrade Kuznetsov would undoubtedly behave like a hero and we would never have the heart to lift a finger against him. In any case, after the initial success we would have been in trouble. There were plenty more suggestions, but my mother-in-law bore the brunt of the work in serving food and drink. Much more of this clandestine activity, I thought in passing, and I would be hard put to it to meet the cost.

At this first meeting I was at last able to meet Ludvík Vaculík in person. He forgave me at once for being the very last man in the country to sign his '2000 Words'. After that we became close friends. Between ourselves we get on excellently; in company we nearly always quarrel, which is supposed to be a sign of good friendship.

At the Olympiad in Lugano Kaválek and I handed our statement to members of the competing teams. FIDE was holding its congress at the same time and a slight incident occurred there in connection with a motion tabled by the Soviet Chess Federation proposing the exclusion of the South Africans from the Olympiad because of their government's denial of human rights. Kaválek and I had addressed a letter to the congress opposing the motion on the grounds that, while we were all against racism and the denial of human rights, the same yardstick should be applied everywhere. When the chairman of FIDE, Dr. Rogard, had shown this to the Soviet delegates, saying that during the debate on their motion he would read it out, they decided not to press for a debate.

On the fourth day in Lugano I was lunching at the Hotel Arozina when the entire Soviet team of eleven came into the restaurant. I greeted them from my table and devoted myself to eating. But suddenly Vasya Smyslov came over to me, saying: 'Luděk, wouldn't you like to sit with us?'

Quite astonished, I said I would be glad to, but what would their political commissar, *Tovarysh* Sherov, say to that. Vasya replied that Sherov himself had sent him. So I picked up my ice-cream and went over to the Soviet table, where Sherov greeted me and almost before I was seated asked if I would be willing to discuss my views. They had heard about my press conference and read the statement—perhaps I would explain it to them. Naturally, I was only too glad to do so. His first question was whether, as a Communist, I agreed that socialism had been in danger of destruction in our country and that capitalism was to have been restored. I replied that there must be some mistake, we were not in favour of capitalism and, anyhow, how could the thing be done, who would have enough money to buy factories and acres of land and so on?

The debate developed, others joined in—members of the Olympic team, old friends of mine. Surprisingly they did not support Sherov, rather the contrary. He was obviously upset. After about three-quarters of an hour he burst out: 'We're your friends, and yet you've killed our soldiers.' I assured him we had not killed a single man, and what was more, not a single shot had been fired by us. He insisted that he had seen the graves of Soviet soldiers who had been killed by our counter-revolutionaries. I informed him that there had indeed been casualties, I could cite a definite case—not far from Prague a Soviet unit encountered some Bulgarian troops at night, and since both thought the others counter-revolutionaries, they fired at each other.

At this Sherov thumped the table, saying: 'Don't you realize the risk your taking? You're sailing mighty near the wind.'

I replied to the effect that I knew it was risky. I had been in prison during the German occupation (I always mentioned that in questionnaires, though it had only been for a few weeks and

I'd have done better to keep quiet about it) and the experience was unpleasant. Nevertheless, I had to stand by my opinions because, after all, not only our nation, but others too were involved. At that point Boris Spassky made a remark which took my breath away—he said: 'That's true, the Czechs are fighting for us too.' My chief partner in the debate then hastened to end the proceedings by declaring, quite incorrectly, that I was very irritable and it was impossible to talk to me. So we took our leave.

When I arrived home from Lugano I found that the atmosphere had changed completely. Depression had vanished, tongues were unloosened, meetings were happening, political life had started again.

In November the Party Central Committee held an important session to discuss the implementing of the Moscow agreement. We knew already that the Action Programme of April 1968, the policy blueprint of the 'Prague Spring', would be to all intents and purposes scrapped and there would be some unpopular personnel changes. On the eve of the session a youth meeting was called in the big Žofín Hall in Prague. The atmosphere was tense at the time: the political weekly 'Reporter' had just been banned and 'press defence committees' were springing up in factories and other workplaces. The day before, Emil and Dana Zátopek and I had signed a 'Declaration in Defence of Freedom of the Press'.

Žofín was packed with young people in militant mood. Emil and I were among the speakers and, at my suggestion, we took the stand together. In replying to questions, I described my debate with the Soviet chess team in Lugano. Strong as my words were, I was lamblike compared with Emil, who spoke of our army 'which hasn't fired a single shot in fifty years', while he renamed the leader of an allied country as Adolf Vissarionovitch Vulbricht [i.e. Ulbricht: a complicated pun which, in addition to the references to Hitler and Stalin, by adding V gave the first syllable of Ulbricht's name the opprobious connotation of 'ox'—translator's note].

17 November saw the start of a student strike in protest against the Central Committee decisions and students occupied

the universities. Strikes in industry also threatened. I was caught up in a whirl of activity—in the eight days between 17 and 24 November, I spoke at seventeen meetings. The last was far away in Moravia. After finishing there at seven in the evening, I set out to drive the 2,400 kilometres to Athens where I was due to play in the international tournament named Acropolis, the first big chess event to be played in Greece.

I had no special ambitions at the tournament, for my head was still buzzing with those passionate meetings. I felt my play to be rather mediocre and I could not be bothered to follow the results. True, I noticed five rounds before the end that Kaválek was two points ahead of me, and the Yugoslav, Ciric, and Bulgarian, Bobotsov, one and a half, so that I looked like ending in fourth or fifth place at best. Then, however, I happened to win three games running. In the fourth I succeeded quite brilliantly in beating Ciric, who aspired to first place. To my astonishment one of the spectators told me that I was in the top three, with a good prospect of winning, because my opponents in the last round were weaker than those Kaválek and Bobotsov had to meet.

The new year opened with a few quiet days until I was invited by the Federation of Youth Organizations to help draft a 'Programme for the Young'. Actually, the idea had originally been mine: young people should have their say in the country's affairs. Then on 15 January there was another big meeting at which a young audience put some pretty odd questions, while the answers, too, often verged on the absurd. For instance, I was asked:

'Mr. Pachman, as a chess player you are well up in the rules of the game, so tell us please whose move it is now.'

On the spur of the moment, I replied: 'We all know quite well who ought to move, but they don't want to.'

To tell the truth, in speaking of those who ought to move, I had in mind the bureaucrats, the incurable dogmatists and all those politicians who were unable to match up to the needs of the day, but the stormy applause showed that my words had been understood in a different sense.

14. The Second Spring and Jan Palach

▪▪▪▪▪▪▪▪▪▪▪▪▪▪▪▪▪▪▪▪▪▪▪▪▪▪▪▪▪▪▪▪▪▪▪▪▪▪

The day following the meeting I spent at home writing. In the afternoon a friend phoned to tell me that a student was reported to have set fire to himself in Wenceslas Square. It was a moment or two before I recalled the demonstrative suicides by Buddhist monks in South Vietnam. The whole thing struck me as strange and unreal. By the evening we had more details, and the student's name: Jan Palach. He was alive—critically ill, but his life might possibly be saved. Most disturbing was the news I heard next day—Jan Palach was not alone, and should his demands not be met, other groups of young people were prepared to follow his example. The demands were two: lifting of press censorship and the withdrawal of foreign troops from our territory. They were not rational demands because censorship was, in practice, almost non-existent, and the withdrawal of troops? How could our Government ensure that? Evidently Jan Palach was a most sincere young man, but lacking in political experience. He wanted to sacrifice himself because all around he saw growing apathy, retreat from ideals, the 'internal emigration' of some, the fatigue of others, and the blatant desertion of the remainder. For all these he wished to offer redemption.

Gradually during the days that followed we began to grasp the whole depth of the tragedy. Again the students went on strike and occupied the universities. I continued the work on the 'Programme for the Young', but it all seemed pointless. Meeting followed meeting. Then, on 18 January, Dr. Bosák, Minister for Youth and Physical Training at that time, asked me to appear on television with an appeal to Palach's friends not to follow his example. This, he told me, was the wish of the President and the

Prime Minister. The talk, which I recorded in Dr. Bosak's office, was as follows:

'Never have I found such difficulty in speaking as at this moment. I am appealing to young people whom I have never met. I appeal to you to desist from an act which I admire profoundly for its moral quality, a deed which has no precedent in our history.

'Believe me when I say that, at this moment, my concern is not merely for your lives, although life is terribly precious and nothing can replace it. I am concerned with the achievement of what both you and I desire. I was among you in the November days, at the Faculty of Philosophy and at many other faculties. Therefore I am sure that you know my views and you know that I, like you, cannot reconcile myself to a life other than that for which we have striven since January; that I refuse to submit to the reality about which we hear so much today; that I believe, with you, in creative unrest. Nevertheless, I am equally convinced that the achievement of our ideals is possible only by the common effort of the fourteen million people of this land, and of many more millions in other lands.

'You feel bound by your promise. I want to say to you that not to keep it will not be cowardly. To live for a great aim can be more heroic than to die for it. But to convince you of that by these few words is an impossible task. One thing, however, I beg of you—get in touch with me, think it over together, and allow me to share with you the experience which you have been unable to acquire. You can rest assured that I shall not betray you, at this or at any other moment of trial.

'My conscience would not permit me to dissuade you from your undertaking if, even for a second, I believed that our cause would be lost without desperate deeds. Yours is a generation destined to live the greater part of your lives in the kind of society we desire. But without people like you, people of true and noble character, without your lives, there is little prospect of our achieving that society.'

Those young people who may recall my speech will probably say that I was lying. For our cause was certainly lost without the desperate deeds, and in all probability it would also have been lost had they been committed.

On the Sunday afternoon, an hour before the start of a meeting at the Natural Sciences Faculty, a student brought the news we had expected and feared—Jan Palach had died. I went straight home after the meeting, arriving as my television talk was ending. They had announced my telephone number, repeating the appeal that Jan Palach's friends should call me. What happened next I recounted in the fifth number of our youth paper, *Mladý svět*, in 1969:

ONE NIGHT'S RECORD
(*Monologue by Luděk Pachman*)

On Sunday afternoon the tragedy was consummated—Jan Palach died. During the first evening transmission of television news I made an urgent appeal to his friends to telephone me and give me an opportunity to talk with them. I wanted to make this attempt to save further lives. A friend warned me, saying that calls would come from everyone except those for whom I would be waiting in hope and despair.

The talk was recorded at midday, and during the evening transmission the announcer gave my phone number. The first call came before the news had ended. That was the start of an evening and a night which I shall never forget, which years hence will still unroll in my mind like a film. Fortunately I made notes, so that I am able to give the precise wording of some of these calls.

A woman's voice begged me with tears to convey her sympathy to Jan Palach's family. Hard on that came the voice of a former colleague anxious to discuss the work of the media—he freed the line at my suggestion that we talk later. A professor from far away in Slovakia wept: 'We Slovaks are overcome with grief and bitterness, he sacrificed himself for us too. I feel as if we had betrayed the Czechs.' Then, following two more calls, one on the subject of politicians 'not wanting to burn their fingers', a hoarse female voice cried hysterically: 'You fascist, you and your like drove him to his death.'

That marked the beginning of the second group of callers which grew, in the subsequent hours, to grotesque proportions. In the meantime, however, an old man, a pensioner, came on the line, his voice choked with tears: 'We have just placed roses for him on the television set. It's a terrible injustice—we can't even move—for three years I've not taken a single step outdoors, but we don't die. Why should a young boy have to die?'

The pace quickened: a housewife, a girl from a newspaper office. Again a woman's voice: 'You'll never get what you want, you rascals!' A doctor, followed by a woman speaking about the psychology of the young. A call from Ostrava expressing grief and sympathy and inquiring about Zátopek. A painter expressed sympathy to the family 'on behalf of all French légionnaires'. Jan Palach, he said, had died for the same ideals for which they had fought and died half a century ago. Hard on this another female voice: 'We'll all be finished, the troops are alerted against us, all because of a few stupid students.' An elderly man: 'Look here, Mr. Pachman, just you stick to your chess and keep out of politics—you don't understand it. Young people are laying down their lives for nothing.'

Then came an interesting question: 'So you've been holding forth again. What will you do when you've lost? The smell of the West comes from you even from the television screen. You and your friends are serving the West. You belong there not here. A year from now we'll talk together in a different manner.'

The first blow came when a girl student from the Faculty of Philosophy announced that she wanted to commit suicide but not publicly. She could live in this world no longer. We talked for some time, finally she promised faithfully not to do it. At that moment I realized I was offering a Samaritan line, a line of trust but also of mistrust. I kept hoping that the people to whom my appeal had been directed would come forward.

A psychoanalyst came on the line. He knew the young generation: one of the causes of the tragedy was the way they had, until recently, been educated, being taught to emulate the heroism symbolized by the Russian sailor, Matrosov, who had silenced an enemy gun with his own body. Bad films in which people threw themselves under tanks were also responsible—that gave a false picture of what heroism is all about. A foreman from an engineering works said: 'Under no circumstances let the young people down, do all you can. We here in the factory helped the students in their strike. I condemn those who have ratted now, in time of trouble.' When I mentioned the unpleasant conversations, he replied: 'In springtime, when the waters flow down, mud moves with them too.' He dictated his name and address.

Now a new round—sad and shocking, an organized campaign of identical calls. Remarkably, almost without exception, they gave impeccable Czech names. The first showed some originality: 'So you want to meet someone—you can meet me, I'll bash your face in.' Those that followed repeated with a remarkable similarity of style the message: 'You've incited people against the Party and the Government, this is the result. Young people have swallowed your criminal propaganda; you've stirred up something which may have incalculable consequences.'

In between, a few pleasant conversations. The trade union chairman at the nuclear research institute left his phone number with an offer to help any effort designed to save lives. A few thank-yous, interrupted by a mother of three: 'You beasts, just because one loony tries to burn himself, you make out it's a national tragedy.'

The apparently genuine Czechs had some error in their private card-index: three accused me of past activity in the Nazi-controlled youth 'Kuratorium'—one added for good measure that I had welcomed Hitler to Prague. Another suggested that I should burn myself with petrol, that being, he alleged, the best death for 'Kuratorists'. Yet another remarked: 'Stalin was right about many things—that's been proved today.'

Around midnight the situation changed. Hitherto the callers had been mainly older people; now the younger, more forceful took over. They seemed to possess a measure of warped intelligence and, perhaps in view of their profession, they showed no sign of needing to go to bed, although one would hardly expect them to be on duty on Sunday. And now the calls were coming at regular intervals. But, much as I would have liked to, I could not unhook the receiver—suppose the lads called and could not get me.

The 'Czechs' recommended that I emigrate immediately, or I would end badly. I clenched my teeth and continued taking the calls. At 2.35 a.m., after being told: 'Just carry on playing chess and don't bother yourself about an idiot who burns himself on Wenceslas Square,' I could take it no longer. I had tried to play the Samaritan; now I could do with help myself.

At seven in the morning I was at the phone again and the roundabout proceeded with mechanical regularity: one call at the hour, another at a quarter past, another at the half hour, and so on. Some did not even speak, others confined themselves to brief remarks such as: 'I just wanted to tell you, you'll be checkmated.' At 8.30 I asked the caller to say a few words, telling him I was recording the conversations and they would be broadcast. The final organized call was at 9.15 and, the campaign being over, private individuals could get through. . . .

At 9.30 I receive the long awaited message. A man's voice says: 'I have to inform you that the only course is for the Government to meet the demands immediately. Otherwise another torch will burn tomorrow.' Uncertain whether this is genuine or a hoax, I put all I have into my reply. At first he refuses, then, at last, he lets himself be persuaded, promising to call again in an hour. The anxious waiting is punctuated by other calls. In the meantime, I write this document, not attempting to smooth things over, just to write it all exactly as it happened—I must not keep this to myself. Uppermost in my thoughts is that precisely organized night-time campaign—they are here, awaiting their opportunity, waiting for their victims. I may be their target now, but they are aiming at all of us. We must not for a moment forget their presence. Let us try to hate them less and understand them more, for that is the only way to counter them. They are not many, but they are highly organized. Though they seem impatient, they evidently want to wait for a year—they keep speaking about a year, or a year and a day. One may have let slip a piece of information when he said: 'We know everything. We have your speeches and letters, we have tapes, too. We shall know how to use them.' I am sure they will know how to use them if their time comes. As yet they are weak, but they hope to grow stronger, they hope that cowards and careerists will join them, especially the cowards. Therefore, we must not, under any circumstances, be afraid. Without courage, we shall die.

Let us try to hate less and understand more.

Now I am waiting. Most important is to save lives. But we should not forget those others, from whom we must save ourselves, and try to save them, too. The latter aim belongs to the human face of the society we want to create.

The days that followed brought strange and puzzling events. I received a phone call from someone claiming to be a spokesman for the 'Palach group'. He said they would not meet anyone for fear of betrayal, but he listened to me and promised to tell them what I had said. To this day I am not sure whether he was genuine or a psychopath of the type well known to criminologists. While four students from the Faculty of Philosophy were visiting me, a professor from the Drama Academy phoned to tell me that number two in the Palach group was a girl now on hunger strike in Wenceslas Square. We rushed to the Square where, in front of the façade of the National Museum, scarred by the gunfire of August, stood tents surrounded by crowds of curious onlookers. The girl, we were told, had just left. Where had she gone? Nobody knew, and we searched for her in vain. But the next day a student leader rang me to say they knew about her and I was not to worry that she would do anything foolish.

Then came the death by burning of Jan Zajíc—in its way a tragedy worse than that of Jan Palach. Palach's deed was a moral challenge, a tragic cry that was rousing because it was unique.

Repetition was impossible. The first name will go down in history, the second will be forgotten.

Suddenly leaflets were circulating in Prague claiming that Jan Palach's self-immolation had been organized by a group of five—Emil Zátopek, Luděk Pachman, writer Pavel Kohout, journalist Vladimír Škutina and student leader Luboš Holeček. We were alleged to have persuaded Palach that the chemical he used would produce 'cold fire'; however, the chemist responsible had made an error in the mixture, hence the tragedy. So we were accused of something compounded of persuasion to commit suicide and murder. How the five names came to be linked I have no idea. Only Pavel Kohout and Emil Zátopek were personally known to me. Pavel had never in his life spoken to Emil, and I first made Škutina's acquaintance when we were invited to speak together at two meetings about this accusation. Incidentally, the macromolecular chemist, Academician Wichterle, stated in the press that there is no such thing as 'cold fire'. It must he thought have been a figment of the imagination on the part of someone who had failed in physics at school.

More serious was that the same 'information' as that in the leaflets was sent by Security to its subordinate offices. Several Members of Parliament were handed the same thing, and Vilém Nový, an old-timer of strong pro-Novotný and pro-Soviet leanings, declared at a meeting in his constituency that the five of us had 'a share in the death of Jan Palach'. The audience booed at this and Nový's wife, who was present, remarked in surprise to her neighbour: 'They don't seem to like Vilém here.' Her husband, upset by the unfavourable reception, announced that he would not be standing for re-election; a statement which was greeted with rapturous applause.

I lodged a charge against Nový, and also against a Security officer who had spread the same 'information'. Then a lawyer, who was an athletics official and friend of Emil's, came to inform me that Zátopek and Škutina were bringing a civil case against Nový—would I join them? I agreed, and I mention this detail because it acquires some significance later in my story.

Early in February I wrote my only really political document of this period, criticizing Prime Minister Černík and other members of our leadership, the 'big five'. Among the stream of articles which I turned out in those days was one in the Catholic paper, *Obroda*, where—for the first time in my life—I wrote about Jesus Christ. It was a great and uncalled for liberty on my part, for I knew little more than that He was crucified under Pontius Pilate and that He gave his life for mankind. In my view, the editors should have sent me packing with that article, but they did not.

The Soviet press and its Czech mouthpiece, *Zprávy*, which was published illegally in our country, had been attacking me since January. 'Soviet Sport' fired the first round with an article headed, 'What about you, Zátopek and Pachman?', which included an assertion that, at the Žofín meeting, I had given an untrue account of my encounter with the Soviet chess players in Lugano. I had said, allegedly, that my arguments had caused the Soviet players to quarrel among themselves until they ended up throwing chess pieces at each other. 'And that is a patent lie,' added the writer, 'because there were no chess sets in the restaurant!' In replying, I wrote that I could confirm this, but I had never said anything about chess pieces. I put it in the form of an open letter to Botvinnik, and I sent copies to the other members of the Soviet team.

Talking of chess, I crossed swords around that time with a section of our national chess leadership. As early as 21 August, in a stormy debate with the chairman, I had told him that either I would end up in jail or he would cease to be chairman. Ultimately, both my predictions were fulfilled. After I had sent a personal protest to FIDE, a statement appeared in 'Czechoslovak Sport' that 'grandmaster Pachman has no authority to speak in the name of Czechoslovak chess players.' I responded with an article in another paper, entitled 'Fear has many eyes' and then, after stormy arguments, I addressed a letter to all district chess clubs, demanding the convening of a full meeting of the organization. This took place in January. The proceedings were lively but, on the whole, unequivocal, with a big majority of

the members supporting me. Consequently, the chairman resigned, thereby bearing out my prophecy of 21 August—the
second part came later.

Then the Soviet papers *Izvestia* and *Literaturnaya gazeta*
joined in the campaign. The former carried an article entitled,
'Dirty play by grandmaster Pachman'. It started with criticism
of an article I had written for the Dutch paper *Het Parool*—of
which more later. Then I was accused of hiding myself under the
'Trojan horse of so-called humane socialism'. The latter
launched a far stronger attack on 2 April, devoting almost an
entire double-page spread to a lengthy piece headed 'Political
gambits of Luděk Pachman'. By way of introduction it mentioned
my book published in Holland and described my alleged entry
into the political arena in August 1968. I had, it seemed, distri-
buted 'to newsagents' my proclamation in which I 'expressed
agreement with the anti-socialist, anti-people "2000 Words"
manifesto which was justly condemned by all honest men as a
counter-revolutionary statement.' I was accused of working for
the CIA, the Pentagon, *émigré* centres abroad and so on. My
reply, in the form of an open letter, was printed in an illegal
paper in the USSR and it was two years later before a copy came
into my possession.

I should explain that the reference to *Het Parool* was occasioned
by the fact that in December 1968 the paper had published a
book entitled 'Seven Days in August', based mainly on a lecture
I delivered at Amsterdam University. Then, following Jan
Palach's funeral, I dictated over the telephone an article which
was printed in *Het Parool* on 28 January 1969. I gave a report of
the funeral and then attempted to analyse the situation in Czechoslovakia. The terrible experience following my television appeal,
and the anonymous letters I had received were still fresh in my
mind. Moreover, there was widespread anxiety that our con-
servatives might make a bid to win power by force, having failed
to come out on top by exploiting the 'Moscow Protocol'. I had
been receiving interesting information on the subject which I
communicated to the political leaders, but unfortunately there
was no response—perhaps it was too much to expect. Anyhow, I

wrote in my article that a political underworld was out to seize power. For this and other statements, the Security police started proceedings against me on 13 March 1969. At first there was no real cause for alarm—I even started a series of articles on the affair in a weekly paper to which I was contributing at the time. I described my initial encounter with the interrogator, Lieutenant Cibulka, adding words of praise for his secretary. When, at the conclusion of my second session, the latter conducted me to the door of the inhospitable building in Bartolomějska Street, she suddenly asked: 'You weren't serious when you wrote that about me, were you?' Since I was unable to recall immediately what I had written, she added that I had described her as 'an attractive secretary'. I assured her that was so, and for that reason I looked forward to the interrogations. She blushed—women are still women, even in the ranks of the Security police!

One disadvantage was that at the start of the proceedings they confiscated my passports, both personal and professional. But I continued to speak at meetings, often travelling considerable distances from Prague. Suddenly I found all sorts of people wanting to talk with me. Usually they were students anxious to have a chat and to be reassured that all was not lost. So I re-assured them although I could have done with reassurance myself. But there were others, too—undoubtedly several police agents among them. One, who introduced himself as a former policeman sacked for criticizing conditions in the force, took me in for quite a time. We were in touch up to my arrest—not that he got much out of me. He cannot have earned much in bonuses, but it was evidently he who, in the summer of 1969, filed the first report about our drafting of the 'Ten Points' petition, to which I shall refer later.

In March came the fateful world championship in ice-hockey. Our victory in the first match was chalked up on all walls, accompanied by slogans, mainly on the theme that the Russian defeat was a revenge for August 1968. Then came the return match. We sat at home in front of the television set. Mrs. Vaculík was with us, Ludvík was expected later. When the final whistle sounded on another victory for our team, we were too excited to stay at home. We drove into the city centre, where the streets were jammed with cars and pedestrians, hooters blared, and people sang and rejoiced. We parked the car and walked to Wenceslas Square, where we were swept by the dense crowd towards the National Museum to the accompaniment of slogan shouting and singing. Ultimately we managed to disentangle ourselves sufficiently to move back down the square and in the lower part we came upon a throng standing in a semicircle in front of the Aeroflot offices. A few lads were throwing stones from a pile lying on the edge of the pavement. Still more remarkable was that not a single guardian of law and order put in an appearance, though they are by no means scarce in our city. We moved on, since throwing stones is not one of our favourite sports. It was a strange night, full of enthusiasm, but also of foreboding.

Next day the Czech Government issued a statement about the demolishing of the office in Wenceslas Square belonging to the Russian airline, Aeroflot, and about disturbances in other towns. It was a dignified and reasonable statement. The trade union daily, *Práce*, asked me to write a commentary on the affair, which I did by first recounting the scene as I had witnessed it, adding that taunts from the crowd directed at the Soviet team were misplaced. From my intimate knowledge of another branch of sport, I could assume that not one of them was guilty of slandering our country. As for the demolition, I was not present when it happened, but it struck me that I might write something about the subject in general.

'We started discussing it', I wrote, 'there in the Square, and one of the debaters drew my attention to the damaged façade of the National Museum. Although there was a certain logic in what he said, it was an incomplete and twisted logic. First, because we shall obviously have to foot the bill both for the façade and the Aeroflot office . . . it is also evident that the attitude to demolishing buildings (or façades) reflects the level of a nation's culture. Truly cultured nations prefer to construct buildings, demolishing them only when they have served their purpose.

'Really I have no idea who started the demolition. Maybe it

was boisterous youngsters, possibly people who had been celebrating by taking a drop too much, or perhaps *provocateurs* who knew what they were doing. I only know that it should not have happened and that for the future we should be careful in our choice of methods. Desiring socialism with a human face, we must under all circumstances behave as human beings, whether matches are lost or won. We can expect to experience many victories and defeats, and not only in ice-hockey.

'This is not just a matter of buildings—democracy cannot be won by undemocratic means. The fight to put decision-making into the hands of decent people does not permit unscrupulous behaviour; resistance to the idea of violence precludes its use except for defence in extremity.'

The day after the article appeared, I was summoned to the *Práce* office. A big row was brewing it seemed. The Soviet Embassy had protested and the Chief Editor was threatened with dismissal and the paper with a ban or a fine. In the event, however, the Chief Editor kept his job until the autumn, and the ban fell on three weeklies—in one case on account of my report about my interrogations. But many newsagents managed to save their supplies from confiscation and, by all reports, they sold at least 70,000 copies.

Alarm spread among journalists. Several of my friends took to ringing me up regularly between four and five in the afternoon. At first I was puzzled, then they told me that they were checking to make sure I was at home. If I was, they could go in peace to their own homes.

Marshal Grechko paid a 'visit' to Czechoslovakia. But he forgot to inform his hosts of his intention. Our Government heard the news when he had already landed at the headquarters of the occupation forces. News of his talks with our leaders leaked out, however. In effect, it was an ultimatum—either put your house in order, or ask us to help you. Grechko considered the situation to be worse than in the months before August 1968. We agreed about that except that we believed that the deterioration was a consequence of August. Cause or effect, that is always the question!

At a big meeting in Liberec, north Bohemia, I informed the audience frankly about these talks, but otherwise I spoke quite mildly. In my view, everything depended on keeping the 'big five' in our leadership together, in so far as it still existed, and I stressed that I meant support for Dr. Husák too. He had been strongly criticized, but I always said that, while I could not agree with his political approach, I considered him to be our most skilful politician. A few days later, however, Dr. Husák delivered an attack on Dubček. He was speaking in the Slovak town of Nitra, and I learnt that the Slovak members of the Central Committee had agreed together to support Husák against Dubček at the pending plenary session. Sixty Slovak votes plus eighty from conservative Czech members meant a clear majority—Dubček's fate was sealed, and that, I was sure, signified the end of the post-January 1968 policies. At last the effects of the August intervention were to be felt. The months of desperate rearguard action were over.

Was there really nothing to be done? On 14 April, I spoke about the Nitra statement and the agreement among the Slovak Central Committee members: 'If we are to describe Dr. Husák's speech in one word, we have to use the word "betrayal". It is a betrayal of the post-January policies.' This earned me, in due course, the charge of defaming a representative of the Republic (under Article 103 of the Criminal Code).

The employees of seventy-two big firms decided to down tools on 17 April and issue a call for a general strike. But the progressive camp was divided, and others felt that to strike would be going too far because it could precipitate the frequently quoted 'incalculable consequences', namely, a second round of invasion and military rule by the occupation forces. My view was that to strike was better than a 'quiet' switch in leadership at the April session because it would rouse the public at home to action and perhaps abroad too. There was even talk about the chances for guerrilla warfare which in the opinion of experts would have been possible for a short period under these conditions.

Some progressives saw Dr. Husák as the saviour, the man who could, on the one hand, placate the Soviet Union and, on the other, preserve the post-January policies. The foremost advocate of this course was Dr. Milan Hübl, one of the authors of the 1968 Action Programme. Now he was lobbying Central Committee members in favour of Husák, thereby offering the waverers and opportunists an excuse for toeing the line when it came to the vote against Dubček. We were indignant, and on the eve of the meeting, Dr. Šabata of Brno, a leading supporter of the Dubček policies and one of the organizers of the Party Congress in August 1968, also gave Hübl a piece of his mind. Not until later did I learn that Hübl was an old friend of Husák who had helped him to return to political life after his spell in prison in the 1950s. In the event, however, neither the ties of friendship nor the help given in April 1969 counted for anything—after Husák's accession to power, Hübl was expelled from the Party, then dismissed from his job, while his wife, too, got the sack. He addressed a pretty stiff open letter to his old friend at the time. Then, in January 1972, he landed in prison where Husák's enemy, Šabata, had been since November 1971. They were brought to trial at about the same time—Hübl got a six-year sentence, Šabata six and a half years. One may recall that Machiavelli wrote about the ingratitude of those who hold power.

To return, however, to April 1969. Owing to disunity, the projected strike was called off at the last moment. I received the news a few hours before the deadline when I was due to speak at the famous ČKD engineering works in Prague, the scene of the August Congress. We called off the mass meeting in favour of a conference among trade union officials, but as I spoke there I was already deeply convinced that our efforts were useless. Then I left for the Faculty of Philosophy where students were arguing with trade unionists about whether or not to strike. Fed up with it all, I went home while they were still talking. I recalled my article in *Christ und Welt* where, after August 1968, I had foreseen a new Battle of Lipany, differing only in its longer duration. Our battle had lasted almost exactly eight months. Now the famous 'salami tactic' had done its job.

Within a few weeks, however, we ventured to make one or two timid moves. People at many workplaces invited journalists,

118

writers and discarded politicians to address them, although the number of us willing to accept was growing smaller and smaller. Yet progressively minded people still headed the trade union branches (even the Communist Party had not been entirely 'consolidated' as an obedient tool), so could something still be saved? Was the Husák leadership somehow open to pressure? There were enthusiasts who wanted to have a try, and I could not be missing from their ranks.

I earned a sharp reprimand from Dr. Husák after a group of us had addressed a mass meeting in the northern industrial centre of Ostrava—we had to hold it out of doors, because the trade union hall had been closed to us by the police. Selecting me from among the other speakers for special attention, Husák declared that while he had no idea what I was like as a chess player, as a politician I was rotten. Today I would be inclined to agree with him, but at the time I was indignant. On impulse I wrote a pamphlet expressing my regret at having maintained that Husák was a good politician, and offering him a lesson in chess because he had 'shown his ignorance of the most elementary rules of the game'. Naturally, the thing was pointless—in politics one must learn not to give way to emotion, and also not to imagine that if the Party boss is free to scold, one can pay him back in like manner.

The last meeting was in mid-July in the town of Rumburk. We went in full force, journalists Škutina, Hochman, Kyncl and myself as well as the popular television newscaster, Kamila Moučková. Here too we found the hall occupied by police, but the local people decided we could meet in a factory. For some two hours the audience of 300 put questions to us until the gate-keeper came running in to say that two police cars were outside, and the officers demanded to be admitted. One of the trade unionists went to deal with the situation, returning after a brief absence to report the following debate at the gates:

They: 'You must let us in.'

I: 'No.'

They: 'What sort of meeting are you holding there? Have you had permission to hold it?'

I: 'I know nothing about a meeting.'

They: 'Come on now, you've got about three hundred people there.'

I: 'Sure, we have some people there, I invited them to tour the works—the trade union has a right to do that.'

At that, they gave up and drove away.

This was the only meeting of which the authorities had no record, whereas they had both reports and tape-recordings of the others. I know because subsequently the commission to consider my expulsion from the Party had to admit that no record was available.

The commission had started work early in July. The first sitting lasted some six to seven hours, discussing everything from Marx to Mao. The concluding minute stated: 'The commission has not succeeded in refuting Comrade Pachman's arguments. The sitting is, therefore, adjourned to allow the commission to be reinforced by ideologically strong members.' When the meeting was reconvened, however, six hours of debating yielded no result. Finally, I was expelled by the district Party committee, meeting in full session after my arrest—in my absence, naturally.

But I have run ahead of the events of that summer. Quite early on some friends and I had decided that we ought to make a clear statement of our views on the way things were going. Aware that a clamp-down on political activity might come at any time, we agreed that the wisest course would be to draw up a petition to be presented to Parliament, the Government and the Communist Party. After all, we had a constitutional right to do so, and as long as we were careful not to circulate the document, we could write what we liked and nothing could happen to us— that, at least, was what we thought.

Our plan was as follows: first we would draft our petition to be signed by about ten initiators who in turn would collect at least five more signatures each. The full list was to be in the nature of a cross-section of the population.

Having gathered suggestions, I made a first draft and we met to discuss it. There was nothing conspiratorial about our choice of meeting place—a club situated on 'Rowers Island' in the middle of the river Vltava, a pleasant enough spot which I suggested in order to spare my mother-in-law the trouble of having a big influx of guests at home. We met there twice during July, once in full force, once with just a few of us. Then my wife and I were due to go on holiday and as the Vaculíks would be staying near us, it was agreed that Ludvík could polish up the draft.

We made the most of glorious weather, bathing every day. Ludvík and I had plenty of opportunity to argue. He insisted that my version of the petition was impossible and since he wanted to transform it into a work of literature, we agreed that after I had gone over the draft again, I would leave the rest to him. Also we hit on a brilliant idea: I had referred to the '2000 Words', but supposing, without any direct mention of past history, we simply issued a petition of precisely 2,000 words?

During the holiday I gave a simultaneous display at which Ludvík was one of the players. About a week later the local chess club invited us to a camp fire at a woodland chalet. As we sat roasting sausages over the fire, the talk turned naturally to politics. There were about fifteen of us there and everyone had something to say, and Ludvík and I were asked numerous questions. In the course of the evening he produced a manuscript I had lent him entitled 'Problems of European Integration and Czechoslovakia'. He wanted me to read it aloud, but I protested that there were about twenty-five pages of it, dull stuff, all theory. In the end, however, I had to comply with the general demand. We sat there until about midnight, we sang some songs and then we drove home. I took the opportunity of handing Ludvík the draft petition.

Back in Prague he brought me his version. I was horrified, because it bore slight resemblance to the original outline. What would the signatories say? But when we met again on 16 August on Rowers Island, after some initial protests, people accepted the new draft with a few slight amendments. Three of the signatories were appointed to put the document into final shape and, to avoid any accusation of trying to stir up demonstrations around 21 August, we would wait until after the anniversary of the invasion before collecting other signatures. In any case things looked like being rather stormy.

By 19 August the scene around our house suggested the imminent outbreak of war. There were two cars up the street and one at our back entrance, all equipped with transmitters. I spent the day at home, working on a chess book due to be handed to the publishers in September. During the afternoon I took a stroll up the hill towards the two cars, whereupon a woman soldier rushed to the transmitting equipment. I approached the plain-clothes men with an invitation to come in for coffee but they refused politely, saying that was not permitted on duty. So I told them that we should be going to the cinema that evening and for their sake we had chosen a detective film. When we set out by car that evening all three vehicles, manned by nine to ten men, were on our tails. The convoy betook itself to the cinema and returned again in close formation to our garage.

Next day, I stayed at home. Dr. Tesař visited me in the evening, and I handed all the petition material to him. We had headed the document, 'Ten Points, addressed to . . .', and attached a list of all the institutions to which it was to be sent. Then followed yet another day at home, although suddenly the coast was clear around our house. Their departure worried me somehow until, when my wife phoned, I realized they had their hands full elsewhere. Things, it seemed, were getting pretty hot in Prague.

We went early to bed. Before going to sleep, I looked through the brown file where I kept a copy of 'Ten Points'.

Almost on the dot of half past midnight, the bell rang. I put my head out of the window to ask who was there.

'Cibulka here,' came the answer.

Hastily I burnt one sheet of paper in the bathroom. I spent five seconds wondering what to do with the 'Ten Points' file, then I pushed it under a cupboard and went to open the door.

Five or six men crowded in. I was to get dressed, they said. They showed me a warrant, according to which I was to be taken into custody on a charge of defaming a representative of the Republic, which act I had committed by virtue of the remarks I had made about Dr. Husák. That struck me as rather ironical—

there had been no lack of speakers attacking Husák at those meetings in the spring. I had been one of the few to underline his good qualities as well. But now I reserved my comments for a later date.

Before I had finished dressing, they were searching the apartment—an operation which took them a full nine hours. They examined everything—all my books and clothes, the sofa, the chairs. The one place they missed was under the cupboard where the 'Ten Points' file was reposing.

On leaving I made a slip of the tongue: 'When the comrades have finished,' I said to my wife, 'don't forget to call in the Cleansing Department.' I had meant to say 'Home Cleaners', the two municipal services being entirely different in their functions. The officer in command protested: 'There's no reason to abuse us, we behave decently.' And so far they really had behaved quite decently.

15. Prison

■.

On arriving at the police headquarters in Bartolomějská Street, I refused to answer questions. Having signed a brief report to this effect, I listened to Cibulka's superior officer remarking, 'We'll have loads of time to talk it over,' after which I was transported to Ruzyň Prison on the outskirts of Prague.

They conducted me to a basement cell where I found sleep impossible because of the strong light shining straight in my eyes. The light shone in the daytime, too, because here in the 'hole' the sun is never seen. The first day in prison started rather gruesomely, with stamping of feet in the corridor, screams and thudding baton blows. Our cell was quiet, we were not taken out for exercise. For breakfast, dry bread and something called coffee.

In the afternoon I was called for questioning. No lawyer attended, but they showed me a statement of some kind according to which the Federal Assembly had issued Decree no. 99 which in effect introduced a state of emergency allowing for three weeks in custody during which I could not even speak to a lawyer. I made no objection to answering questions, however, because the case seemed quite simple and my defence obvious. I had two arguments: first, I had referred to Dr. Husák in terms approximately as strong as those he used about me and, after all, citizens are equal under the law. Second, the Article of the Criminal Code about 'defaming a representative of the Republic' could not apply to Dr. Husák since he represents a political party, the Communist Party, not the Republic. I could cite the precedent of *Jindra* v. *Dr. Pus* in 1965. The parties to this case, after a prelude consisting of rum or slivovitz, had agreed together in ringing tones that Antonín Novotný was an utter . . . (here came the incriminating epithet). Defence counsel was at pains to prove the precise time when the words were spoken. The reason for his attention to what appeared to be a technical detail emerged during his winding up. He argued that the 'defaming' had occurred at a time when Novotný was not yet President—he had been elected, but had not taken the oath of office, therefore he was still no more than a representative of a political party. Although the court sent learned counsel packing with this defence, an acquittal was obtained on appeal to the Supreme Court. It seemed to me impossible that Dr. Husák's name would be even more strictly protected than Novotný's—so why was I in prison? Naturally, I would raise objections.

For eight days there were three of us in the basement cell. The toilet in the corner was of the standing-up type, with no screen. I introduced the custom that the two non-toilet users discreetly turned their backs, but in any case it was far from cosy. Later I hit on the idea of using a small iron stool we had in the cell to provide a seat, thereby solving one serious problem. I also lodged a complaint that, in contravention of prison regulations, we had no exercise. I was told that this was due to the over-crowding with hooligans who had been driven by people like myself to demonstrate on 21 August against Party and State.

My three weeks' detention was about to end when I succumbed to a bad attack of intestinal catarrh. The doctor transferred me to Pankrác Prison hospital for examination. On my very first day there Mr. Cibulka turned up. Instead of replying to my query whether he had come to release me, he shoved a piece of paper into my hand. From it I read that I was charged with subversion on a large scale under Article 98 (2) of the Criminal Code, an offence carrying a penalty of two to ten years' imprisonment.

I goggled unbelievingly at the paper, noting among other things that I had exerted an anti-State influence in the trade unions, I had disrupted morale in the factories, and so on. The charges amazed me and, above all, they made me angry. Immediately I wrote complaints in all directions, including a personal letter to the President. Then I announced that I was going on hunger strike. My defence lawyer, to whom I now spoke for the first time, tried to dissuade me, but then he promised to inform my wife. I maintained the strike for exactly four weeks—for the first two, I took no nourishment, then, on doctors' advice, I agreed to artificial feeding three times a week. A record was written that this measure did not affect the continuance of the hunger strike as a form of political protest. Thanks to this, my life was not endangered and I lost only 17 kilogrammes in weight. On promising to try to persuade me to abandon my action, my wife at last received permission to visit me.

The Prosecutor-General's office responded to my complaint by informing me that the charges had been withdrawn. Surprise and rejoicing? Unfortunately, no—a second document was enclosed, laying a new charge against me, the third since my arrest. This time it referred to the organization of illegal meetings on Rowers Island and at the woodland chalet with intent to threaten the consolidation of affairs in our Republic and to provoke a seditious campaign with the aid of subversive matter known as the 'Ten Points'. The whole thing was beyond me, but I now stood to get a sentence of 'only' one to five years in prison.

Having ended the hunger strike, I was taken back to Ruzyň, to a cell on the sixth floor. The accommodation was quite luxurious with a proper bed and a toilet with a seat. I had two companions, Emil and Pavel, one charged with murder, the other with breaking and entering and theft.

For several weeks I was not called for interrogation. Having been sent a chess set from home, I occupied myself with studying some variations. I also churned out a stream of letters since in those days prisoners were still allowed to correspond at will, and most of my letters reached their destinations. Friends and relations wrote to me and, to my surprise, even some discreet political allusions got through. Dana Zátopek pasted pictures of towns on her letters—I was meant to guess the names, but I discovered by unsticking the photos that the names were printed on the back, so I was able to amaze Dana by getting them all right.

We went to bed early. At 7 p.m. one was allowed to lie down, at 9 came 'lights out', meaning you had to be in bed, although the lights shone all night. Someone used to shout: 'To all boys and girls in Ruzyň, good-night from Piggyyyy!' Once he went one better: 'To all murderers and tarts, thieves and frauds, and political secretaries, too, good-night from Piggyyyy!'

Then other voices sounded through the courtyard. For instance: 'Tonda calling Franta, hullo old cock, are you there?'

'I'm here, what's up, cock?'

'Hi, I bashed that lorry, so mind you don't blab!'

A warning shot from the guard would impose a brief silence, then more shouting. The chief purpose of detention was to prevent accomplices from communicating with each other, and this provision of the Criminal Code was cited in my case. But with whom and about what might I communicate? The 'Ten Points' could be read by all. My lawyer told me that after my arrest the document had been delivered, with all our signatures, to the list of institutions. Subsequently, evidently by way of reply to our petition—in the manner sometimes used by feudal lords—two of the signatories, Battěk and Tesář, had been taken into custody.

Towards the end of November or it may have been early December, I sensed something odd about my cell-mate, Pavel. He was frequently called for interrogation, but could offer us no proper explanation of what they wanted from him. He produced a fantastic story about having run away to France, and now he was being questioned about co-operation with the French Intelligence Service. One day I simply grabbed him by the collar, looked him straight in the eye and asked him to come clean. Soon he broke down in tears and it came out that he had been promised a shorter sentence if he would ask me about certain matters, then sign his name to a report of what I had said. A quarter of an hour after this talk two warders burst into the cell and literally carried Pavel away.

The incident upset me—obviously, the cell was bugged, and I kept worrying about all the things I might have said. True, I could recall nothing of any real importance, but tapes can always be pieced together to suit any purpose. So far my spirits had been exemplary—every day I had sung, 'My little country', with special emphasis on the words '. . . again and again, she will

127

blossom, my country!', and I had told, and even invented, political jokes. Now I was tongue-tied, losing faith in Emil, too. This upset him so much that, one day, he shook me, yelling, 'Sod it, what's got into you?'

Early in December I was questioned for the first time about the 'Ten Points'. That held no worries, but during the session I was in a strange state—at times it was as if I was listening to myself, as if someone else was speaking. Perhaps it was due to having had no one asking me about anything for weeks on end. On the third day I had to dictate my life history. I laid it on thick, stressing that I had been imprisoned by the Gestapo and that a partisan commissar had been quartered in my home. As soon as I was back in the cell, I felt quite sick—what was the point of chattering like that, it would look as if I was trying to make capital out of past services. Later, I demanded permission to rewrite my life history, and I cut all that out. During these interrogations I also learnt that the 'Ten Points' petition had been broadcast by Radio Free Europe and other stations, and it had appeared in several newspapers.

A week later came the so-called acquainting of the defendant with the results of the investigation. I was able to read the statements by witnesses and to re-read my own statement—in all, it was a mountain of paper. I was thunderstruck by what some of the witnesses had said. Two, for instance, 'recalled' how I had read out the 'Ten Points' to everyone round the camp fire on that evening at the chalet. How so, since the document had not even been completed at the time? Others insisted I had read something quite different. Then, when I came to the testimony of Emil Zátopek, my friend for twenty years, I was unwilling to believe my eyes. I read it through several times, and some passages are so clearly imprinted on my memory that I can quote precisely. For instance: 'In June 1969 the Soviet chess player, Keres, visited Pachman in his apartment. Pachman asked Keres whether he would like to emigrate from the Soviet Union and Keres replied by asking whether Pachman had considered emigrating from Czechoslovakia.'

What had actually happened was that in June 1969 Keres and

Korchnoi played for the Soviet Union at a tournament in Luhačovice. I had refused to play in view of the Soviet participation. But despite this demonstration on my part, I had wanted to show that the players were still my personal friends. So I had gone to watch the tournament and we had had a friendly talk. In Prague, I invited them home to supper, but as Korchnoi was unable to come, I had invited Emil to take his place. And what was this talk about emigrating? Vaguely I recalled that we had talked about cars. Keres was having some difficulty in getting spare parts for his American-made automobile, and no one in Russia, he complained, was capable of repairing it.

'Well, there's nothing for it but to emigrate with that Ford of yours,' I remarked jokingly, and he responded in the same tone, saying, 'Come with me, if you like, there's plenty of room for two!'

Whatever had happened to Emil? Keres could get into trouble over this, and he was completely innocent. Since they never asked about the incident during interrogation, I had no chance to put the record straight, so that is how it stands in the documents.

On returning to the cell, I confided in the other Emil. His response was simple: 'Well, just bugger the sod!'

Now that the investigation was completed, my lawyer entered a proposal for my release from custody, which gave me a faint hope of being home by Christmas. The reply was not long in coming: application for release refused. Inconsistencies (what were they?) in the statements require that the case be referred for further examination.

My last clear memory from the days before Christmas is of Emil and myself secretly burning newspaper in the cell in order to make instant coffee. Then followed mornings when I woke at two or three, soaked with sweat and shivering as if with fear, but I was not afraid. The strangest thoughts kept running through my mind—for instance, that I would die on Christmas day. Emil cried out in despair: 'Sod it, has that bloody Zátopek knocked you right out?' But quite different matters were passing through my mind.

Of what followed I can give no connected account because I

would be reporting what other people have to say about it. I remember being transferred to another cell and waking in the morning on a straw bed with an acute pain in my back. Then I was taken to hospital where they X-rayed me and told me that in the night I had rammed my head against the wall. My response was to say that in the Middle Ages knights condemned to death used to kill themselves in this manner, and in return for saving the executioner his work, their property could remain with their families. That idea struck me when they told me about jumping at the wall, but I am certain I never wanted to kill myself in that manner.

As I lay in hospital, unable to lift my head, I saw my wife sitting by the bed and the Prosecutor standing near by. It seemed she had been allowed a visit that day, but when she and the Prosecutor (who had to be present at every visit) arrived at Ruzyň, they learnt that I was in hospital. When they left the doctor came to tell me that I had a cracked skull and an injury to my spine.

Towards the end of January, Lieutenant Cibulka appeared in my room. He informed me that the investigation would proceed, but first I would be transferred to the prison department of the psychiatric hospital at Bohnice near Prague. I objected that I felt quite well, and I had not tried to commit suicide. In the end I withdrew the objection on the advice of my defence lawyer, who pointed out that resisting the order would merely prolong the investigation and, consequently, my term of detention.

Examination lasting nearly two months at Bohnice concluded with the doctors pronouncing me of sound mind. My strange symptoms, showing features of paranoia, were, apparently, induced by detention psychosis. My IQ was 140—not bad, it seems, considering I have no university education.

Interrogations continued all the time. They were obviously being intentionally prolonged in the hope of getting me to disassociate myself from the 'Ten Points' and win my release—but I pretended not to understand. So by the end of March I was back in Ruzyň, and in April we had the 'acquainting oneself with the results of the investigation' again. By now I figured as the head of a group, so the case bore the name 'Case of Pachman and others'.

My main interest was when the trial would take place. Serving a sentence is paradise compared with pre-trial detention—one has some freedom of movement, and can work instead of having to stare all day long at the walls of a cell. That, at least, was what I thought, but friends told me later that the work is usually none too pleasant. The state of affairs in our prisons altogether surprised me. I had never been inside in another country, but I had read about prison conditions. The usual practice is for things to be easier for people held in custody before trial, when their guilt has not yet been proved. In our country the reverse is true: you have minimum rights and privileges under pre-trial detention— to watch television or listen to the radio, for instance, is unheard of. I read that Angela Davis protested on one occasion that they had taken away her transistor radio; I can inform her that I never once listened to the radio when I was in prison. The only comparison I could make was with Mladá Boleslav in 1940, under the Gestapo. There was less food then, of course, but food was short everywhere in those days. Otherwise, things were much better— the cell was a palace compared with the present one, with a proper flush lavatory and a normal bed. We had an hour's exercise daily, walking in a big circle, whereas this time the occupants of each cell were put separately into concrete enclosures, known to us as calf-pens. Why was the Gestapo less vigilant than our guardians of today?

However, all this could be borne—worse was the utter lack of activity. The Penal Code limits pre-trial detention to two months, to be prolonged only with good cause. Now I had been held for no reason at all for four times the permitted term, and the end was not in sight. Towards the end of April I spent another week in Pankrác Prison hospital, then I was transferred to a cell. My companion's profession of stool-pigeon could be smelt a mile off. Since he played chess not at all badly, he must have been specially picked for the job. Having told him I knew why he was with me, I suggested the following: for lack of any other occupation, we would play chess, and I would talk about the weather

131

and girls, while it would be up to him to think up reports to satisfy his bosses. He took the situation in a sporting spirit.

While I was in hospital I had asked my wife to send me a Bible, which, after some demur, was permitted by the authorities. Now I started serious reading. It was hard going especially with the Old Testament. I made notes and also a list of questions I would like to put to a priest. Twice I prayed in my cell. On the first occasion a warder opened up the cell and said, laughing: 'Sure, you save your soul, that's the main thing.' The second time, the warder looked through the peep-hole and asked what I was doing. I replied that I was praying and thinking about life—the word meditation did not yet come naturally to me. Quite amiably, it seemed to me, he told me to go ahead.

Again I received notice that I was to be 'acquainted with the documents', my term of detention was extended, my objections to custody rejected as groundless. This was, of course, a direct invitation to capitulate and repent. When I found nothing new in the record, apart from a few trivialities, I was seized with doubt—perhaps this was all a sham. There must be something else in the case because it was really impossible to prolong detention so long on such insubstantial charges. The idea gripped me more and more—in the end, I decided to go on hunger strike again. That started a silly cat-and-mouse business. I was forced to accept meals and leave them on the table because when I refused, a warder would burst into the cell and behave very roughly. After a week of this, my lawyer persuaded me to call it off on the grounds that the case was bound to come to court at any moment —the hunger strike would simply prolong the detention of my colleagues and myself unnecessarily.

One day I was, indeed, taken to the law courts—to attend the civil law hearing in the case against Vilém Nový. Outside the court-room I saw my wife and a neighbour; inside I recognized a couple of friends. Then Emil Zátopek came up to say hullo and shake hands, but my bodyguard hastily shooed him away.

The hearing was a farce—Nový made no attempt to deny the words ascribed to him, he simply declared that the five of us who were suing him bore political responsibility for all evils and, consequently, for Jan Palach's death as well. But Emil Zátopek caused a sensation, which the press took up in a big way next day. He announced that he had never meant to sue Nový, his friends had persuaded him. Now he realized that his attitude would imply hostility to socialism and, since that was not his intention, he asked Nový's pardon and withdrew his suit. Then Emil went over to Nový, his hand extended—it looked as if they were about to hug each other in a 'double Khrushchev', but they merely shook hands. At this, Pavel Kohout rose to demand that the court take note that he had never in his life spoken to Zátopek, therefore he could not have persuaded him. Holeček said something to the same effect—in short, I was obviously the guilty party and, of course, the judge rejected our plea.

Back in prison, my sole companion was the stool-pigeon. We took our exercise alone (but with a warder, of course) in a garden where nobody ever came. By the end of August I was in pretty bad shape. I would lie on my bunk with the strangest thoughts chasing through my head. I stopped playing chess, I stopped reading, I simply gazed into space. Then I started the hunger strike again. This time without any announcement, I just stopped eating. Again they transferred me to hospital, where I stopped drinking as well. So they started force feeding, prying my mouth open with a metal instrument and shoving a tube down my throat. I found resistance was futile, but I tried to keep my mouth shut. Then they informed me that they were not equipped for force feeding, so I was to be transferred back to the prison department in Bohnice mental hospital—this time not for examination of my mental state, but for treatment. That, however, failed to materialize, and all they did was to leave me sitting in a cell. After an unsuccessful attempt by my lawyer to get me to call it off, they introduced feeding through the nose three times a day. I was very weak, and I developed a pain in the area of my kidneys and bladder. By October I weighed 56 kilogrammes, 32 below my normal weight. At that point I was told that the trial was about to be held, but that I would be tried separately when I was well.

Finally, in the afternoon of 19 October, a gentleman visited me, saying he came from the City Court. He handed me a paper announcing that I was to be released because the grounds for my detention no longer applied. Continuation of criminal activity by the accused was not to be expected in view of his state of health and the degree of political consolidation now achieved in the country. The accused would be transferred to the civilian section of Bohnice hospital.

As I stared at the paper, it was all one to me. Then someone helped me to get dressed and took me out to where my wife was waiting—not to take me home but to another part of the hospital. There I still felt no desire to eat—in any case, this was internment, not release—so the prison doctors continued to feed me, but in bed without compulsion. I decided I ought not even to look at the world, certainly I should not talk, so I shut my eyes and, except for one fleeting moment, I never opened them until I had really left the place. In time, I started communicating with my surroundings by writing with my eyes shut. This I did even when my wife visited me, and we still have the bits of paper stored away at home. Listening to the transistor radio she brought me, I had my first chance in fifteen months to enjoy some music. And as for food, when I decided to start eating, I had everything the heart could desire: they consulted me every morning about the menu.

Euženie told me about the efforts my friends abroad had made on my behalf. What had upset me most in prison was the thought that people had washed their hands of me, that they did not care if I rotted there. Now I began to take some interest in these matters, but I still kept my eyes shut and refused to communicate except in writing. Finally, on 9 December, the doctor asked me if I would open my eyes and speak after discharge from hospital. I wrote: 'Of course, at home I shall speak and open my eyes.' Then they led me into the passage, my wife embraced me, I opened my eyes and saw her for the first time since she had fetched me from the prison section.

My mother-in-law welcomed me home with an excellent meal of chicken, then I settled comfortably in an armchair. Almost sixteen months had passed, everything seemed strange, somehow unreal. Our sitting-room was like a big hall, the light was curiously yellow.

Next day Dick Verkijk telephoned from Amsterdam—he was the Dutch journalist who had been deported from Czechoslovakia on the pretext that he was a 'spy'. He asked me for a short interview, which I gave, but we left politics out of it. I thanked friends in Holland for their solidarity—I had found hundreds of letters from that country awaiting me at home. Children from the Anna Frank school in Utrecht had sent me a collection of their drawings, half of which had been delivered to me in prison, the rest I had now received. The pictures in this second batch were mainly about prison life—a prisoner with a ball and chain on his leg; a wicked warder standing over him with a stick; and another in two parts—on one side a Czechoslovak flag with a prisoner in striped clothing beneath it, on the other a Dutch flag flying over the heads of people who were surrounded by tulips. The ones sent to me in prison were designed to cheer me up. Now I was able to thank the children over the radio.

Soon friends started dropping in, at first anxious to know if they were not disturbing me, then more frequently, without apologies. Life was back to normal.

16. A New Faith

On one of the first occasions that I ventured out of the house, I visited the parish priest of our district. Having explained that I had left the Church in 1946, I said I now wished to return because I believed in God. When I had shown my birth certificate, I was told that the Bishop would have to decide what to do. Nothing could be done before Christmas, but perhaps, if the Bishop agreed, I could be admitted to confession before the New Year, after which everything would be in order.

When I discussed the matter with Ludvík, he said that he, too, was close to believing in God, but on my proposal to return to the Church he commented dryly: 'You always have to belong to some party, don't you?' We debated the question of what is and what is not a party, which landed us, after the long interval, in a good quarrel.

In answering the question, why?—which, of course, cannot be avoided—I am conscious that I still know very little and, in any case, it is difficult to explain. The existence of God is an idea which has been surfacing in my mind on and off for the last twenty years or so. My leaving the Church in 1946 was a matter of course—obviously there was no God, religion was 'the opium of the people', the weapon of obscurantists and exploiters. By 1947 I was giving classes on dialectical and historical materialism, the book by J. V. Stalin bearing this title being my chief source of wisdom. How simple and easy to understand it was! Just knowing all that was written there, with perhaps a little extra, one could answer all questions. I felt that the time was near when everyone would see the light, realize what they should do, and join us on the forward march.

When I was in hospital in February 1948 having my Achilles'

tendon operated on, I experienced a curious sensation as they gave me the anaesthetic—the thought struck me, this is God! On waking up I murmured something about Buddha—why the name occurred to me, I have no idea. Of course, I told myself, one can have hallucinations under anaesthetic. I made a note of my sensations, however, with a view to asking experts for their views, but then I lost the notes. Then one lovely spring afternoon, having fallen into a doze, I had the same feelings again, so much so that I was frightened into dragging myself out of my half-sleep. I never told anyone about these experiences, and for some time I stopped thinking about them. Life was a hectic round of chess tournaments, meetings, plans, friends. Nevertheless, by the 1950s, and still more in the early 1960s, I began to question whether dialectical materialism was really the last word in wisdom, offering the ultimate truth. I became interested in Einstein's relativity theory. I learnt from books on physics that an electron can be in two places at once—the principle of uncertainty and all the rest of it finished me. Matter was the basis of everything, yet no one knew what it really was—if anything is certain, it is that the concept of matter is extremely uncertain.

Soon I was proclaiming to all and sundry that dialectical materialism was an outlived theory and the Communist movement would manage quite well without it. After all, most important in Marxism are the economic parts and some of the sociological findings. Does everything have to be meticulously rounded off, people's thinking arranged for them with no question left unanswered? Why could not socialism, as a just and properly functioning society, tolerate a diversity of philosophical systems? My idea was that Communism could, and one day would, discard what I had suddenly found to be a simplified and vulgarized approach. I liked the proposition that a little philosophy leads to materialism, more philosophy to idealism. When biology was being debated in the Soviet Union, I spoke quite openly against their idol, the agricultural theorist, Lysenko, and no one in authority tried to silence me. Presumably, as long as I was against imperialism, they could tolerate my harmless madness.

In short, I have been a confirmed materialist for about one-tenth of my membership of the Communist movement. I hoped that its total identification with materialism would not be lasting, but should the change not come, I knew that communism could attract me no more, although I saw little chance for socialism apart from this movement—whether Labour parties win or lose elections makes little difference.

When I started praying I am not sure, but it was at a tournament somewhere; I needed something from God, probably I had an important game to win. I also went into a church on several occasions, just to sit and meditate and repeat the few prayers I remembered from childhood. My first conversation with Eužénie about belief in God was during one of her visits to Pankrác Prison sometime in July 1970. She was surprised, but she thought about it. Then I wrote to her on the subject, and when I got home, I confided everything, at least everything I felt sure about. For during those dark nights in Pankrác and Bohnice I had discovered things confirming my experience in 1948. And from Christmas 1970, we started going to church regularly.

Eužénie decided that she wanted to be baptized, so Ludvík's wife, Madla, took me to see her confessor. In the course of our conversation, on hearing that we had been married in 1946 and would be celebrating out silver wedding in September, the priest pointed out that, even at this late date, we should solemnize our wedding in church, otherwise we could not receive the sacrament. So we arranged to hold the ceremony on 6 September, our silver wedding day, in Týn Church on Prague's Old Town Square.

17. Banned from Chess

In Ruzyň Prison, and also in the Bohnice hospital, I had often thought how nice it would be to be really and truly playing chess again, to be battling at a tournament, to be excited over a contest with Bobby Fischer perhaps, to rack my brains over how to move 1 P–K4. So now I decided to try my luck. After all, I had accomplished something in chess, my name still meant something, perhaps I was still capable of having a go at it. And the gentlemen in the seats of power ought to be glad if I turned again to chess instead of politics. The chess officials were my old friends, I had helped many of them in the past—the general secretary, Šajtar, for instance, knew how I had backed him for his international posts.

Without delay I wrote on 28 December to ask the Federation about my prospects. I was willing to give an undertaking that I would not mix chess with politics in any way whatsoever.

The reply came fairly promptly, and it was brief:

Dear Comrade,
We acknowledge your letter of 28 December 1970, which was considered by the Executive Committee of the Czechoslovak Chess Federation at its meeting on 8 January 1971. In view of the standpoint of the Training Council, with which it concurred, the Executive has concluded that by your attitude and statements made during 1968 and 1969 you disqualified yourself from membership among the national representatives of our socialist sport. The position remains unchanged.
Yours etc.
Božětěch Vránek, Acting Chairman CCF;
Jaroslav Šajtar, General Secretary CCF.

So there was a new chairman. When they took me off to Ruzyň, the post was still held by General Macek who, on the first anniversary of the invasion, led a demonstration down Wenceslas Square wearing his general's uniform although he was already on the retired list. Vránek, too, was an old friend, but he had formerly worked at the Ministry of the Interior, which obviously made him more reliable than his predecessor.

I lodged a complaint with the Executive of the Sports Union stating that I had done nothing to disqualify myself and, what was more, the disciplinary rules only allowed for penalizing offences dating back less than six months. Ludvík, when he read the official letter, was so incensed that he set to that evening to write on his own account. Having thrown away five drafts (there he differs from me—I write everything straight off and other people throw out the results for me), at three in the morning he produced the following:

Messrs. B. Vránek and J. Šajtar
Gentlemen,
My friend Luděk Pachman has shown me your letter informing him that he has been expelled from national representation in chess. You say that he expelled himself by virtue of his views and attitudes in 1968–9. I am writing to you because your letter concerns me, because everything concerns me. Moreover, I too play chess, badly, but with enjoyment. Chess, gentlemen, oh yes, it is a royal game, isn't it?

Your letter, on the other hand, is rude and conceited, and the thinking behind it is simple-minded in the extreme. It is as if it had been written by someone who, even in a leisure moment in the safety of his home, has never thought about life except in the manner of a petty official ever anxious about his daily bread. But one must know how to differentiate! Obviously, a political battle, where the winning side may unseat its opponents for a time, is one thing—there we have the accepted morality of politics and power. But quite another matter is human decency, cultured sensitivity and the sporting spirit, which are inviolable. Therefore you should take note that the overwhelming majority of the nation condemns those who take advantage of the present situation to conduct, on the pretext of continuing the political battle, what is essentially a dirty careerist campaign against people with divergent views, and who use whatever influence they possess to carry the persecution into workplaces and private lives. They employ for this purpose the type of people who are willing to serve them. But why does the chess organization have to join in?

You have expressed your disagreement with Pachman's views only after your superiors moved against him—the men who at any moment may sweep you aside, too. Therefore, I suspect that cowardice prompted you to write your letter. Let your elder children assure you that a man holds opinions in order to act on them, so long as he does not thereby infringe the law of laws and the dictates of his conscience. And he who forbids a man to act on his opinions forbids him to live as a human being. Why do you join in this?

You have no authority to act in this manner. You decide bureaucratically whether or not Pachman shall play international chess, although plain common sense shows that the decision is his, to be made in honourable contests. Indeed, in your better moments, that must be clear to you. Have you asked the members of your union for their views on the matter? Does whoever you approached for advice know how to play chess? Or do you, perhaps, regard Pachman as your property? Even were that to be so, you ought, presumably, to look after him so that he can develop! From your letter I must presume that you will start laying down which combinations in chess are politically acceptable in order that 'all the people' may understand them. Just as restricting art to what is comprehensible to everyone means destroying art completely, so your chess policy can lead to the complete destruction of the game. Consequently, I would not be surprised to find Czech players refusing to sit down to the chessboards, and foreign players expressing their contempt. The chessboard is, of course, governed by the monarchist principle and organized in a military manner, but the fact that the principle and the organization have to be obeyed by all who sit down to the board makes it incomparably more democratic than anything in our set-up. Once, in a village inn, I saw a drunken bully go up to a pair of chess players. For a while he swayed ominously over the board, then, with besotted muttering, he picked one piece at random from each player and made off with them. On reading your letter, gentlemen chess officials, I recalled that incident.

Ludvík Vaculík

Copies to: *Luděk Pachman*
    Prosecutor-General—notifying commission of the criminal offence of oppression (Article 237, Criminal Code);
    Czech National Council—notifying damage to state interests abroad;
    Ministry of Culture—notifying anti-cultural behaviour.

In due course Ludvík received a reply from the Prosecutor-General's office stating that grounds for action were lacking.

Towards the end of February 1970, I was invited to appear before the Appeals Commission of ČSTV (Czechoslovak Union of Physical Training). I sat alone on one side of the room, with some ten men facing me in a semicircle, of whom only the secretary was known to me. Presiding over the proceedings was a white-haired gentleman, precise in statement and forceful in delivery. He addressed me as follows:

'In the years 1968–9, you frequently employed the term occupation to describe the events of August 1968. Why did you do so and would you employ that term today?'

I expressed my surprise that instead of discussing my chess activities, they had thought fit to examine me in history or politics. If I was to be examined, however, I was bound to say that I would still employ the term—and I quoted the dictionary definition of occupation as signifying taking possession of the territory of a foreign state.

A confused debate followed, during which the white-haired

gentleman plied me with questions extracted from a fat file on the table before him. When this had been going on for about three hours, he fired this broadside:

'During a full two and a half years you have not once condemned the Israeli aggression against the Arab countries?'

I had been expecting something of the sort, although in a somewhat more intelligent form. I replied that I was unable to condemn because by so doing I would come into conflict with the definition of aggression tabled by the Soviet Union at the United Nations. By this definition, the aggressors in 1967 were the Arabs. My explanation was then cut short by the chairman, who exclaimed:

'Enough! That's all we need, we have a clear picture now.'

So I thanked them for their attention and left for dinner. In due course I received an intimation in writing that the decision of the Chess Federation had been confirmed. I was a bit surprised by what struck me as a stupid way of doing things, but later I discovered that I was no exception, nor had I, by the standards of the time, been unduly persecuted. At the so-called work check-ups one's attitude to August 1968 was crucial, a man's fate hung upon it. There was an anecdote current in Prague—the scene, a check-up session:

Question: Do you regard August 1968 as an act of fraternal aid or as the occupation of our country?
Answer: Fraternal aid, of course!
Question: When did you arrive at this view?
Answer: On the very first day of the occupation!

Thousands had to change their jobs—the worst sufferers being journalists and intellectuals of all kinds, including many eminent scholars. The new occupations of those lucky enough to find employment included quarrying, bulldozer driving, stoking and other manual work. My wife was dismissed on 1 October 1970 from her job in physical training, having been previously expelled from the Party at a stormy meeting called specially to deal with her. The reference they gave her abounded with praise for her abilities, her devotion and initiative, with a brief statement in

143

conclusion to the effect that, since she had refused to retract her mistaken views, it was necessary to end her employment.

Armed with this reference, she spent two months applying for work at various factories, with no success until, by some miracle, a small co-operative firm agreed to take her on—at a wage considerably lower than her former salary.

I heard a joke about a certain Prague works where these two labels were affixed to two neighbouring cupboards in the cloak-room:

Prof. Dr. . . . ., D.Sc., stoker

Prof. . . . ., B.Sc., assistant stoker

Which suggests that qualifications were not entirely ignored— the higher academic degree ensured a slightly higher position on the works ladder!

Despite these experiences, I persisted in my efforts to get back to the chessboard—without publicly retracting my views, of course. First I had to find out what 'expulsion from national representation' actually meant. Obviously I was barred from playing for the national team and in official competitions. But did the ban also apply to tournaments where I would play solely on my own behalf? Three invitations to tournaments—in Sarajevo, in Israel and in Puerto Rico—I sent to headquarters with a request for permission to travel. The refusal came with the stereotype explanation that these tournaments did not figure in our plan for international events. But I discovered that, while making this excuse to me, our Federation had offered the Yugo-slavs the participation of 'another Czechoslovak player'.

So international events were out, but not, for the time being, home events. Moreover, the ČSTV rules expressly distinguish between a 'ban on national representation' and a 'ban on playing in international club events'. Perhaps, then I would be able to play for my club in international matches. Things might not be so hopeless after all.

I played on first board for my club in the national teams championship, where my performance was average, but I hoped I would be able to regain my form within a few months. I tied with Hort, which intrigued some onlookers. At an international tournament in Luhačovice, I had an interesting encounter. Vaculík and I had gone there as spectators and to see some of our friends from various countries. Arriving at midday, we went to a restaurant and the waiter ushered us into a separate room where the chess players were having lunch. We were still in the doorway when the Soviet grandmaster, Antoshin, leapt to his feet and made a rapid exit, leaving half his meal and an untouched glass of Pilsner beer on the table. The other Soviet representative, Liberzon, on the contrary, rose with complete composure, held out his hand and replied to my inquiry about the health of his brother with whom I had exchanged gramophone records in 1968. Later, in the tournament hall, he exchanged a few words with me in the presence of onlookers. Other players—Hungarian, Bulgarian, and even a chessmaster from the German Democratic Republic, talked freely with me, as with an old friend, not a criminal.

When his game ended, I had a talk with Laszlo Szabo with whom, in October 1968, I had spoken for the *Deutsche Welle* transmission to Hungary. I had little fear that he had suffered any consequences back home, since their top man, Kadar, has a soft spot for chess players. Vaculík was with me, so I introduced him to Szabo, who laughed and said that here was the whole Czech counter-revolution. We laughed, too, as we returned to the tournament hall, where I noticed our new chairman, Božětěch Vránek walking around. In a while, he came up to us, offering me his hand with a sweeping gesture and uttering a jovial 'Hullo!'—probably he thought he was doing me a favour. I gazed into space beyond him, roughly in the direction of the demonstration chessboard, and he, his hand slowly dropping, exclaimed: 'Luděk, don't you know me any more?'

'I don't believe we are acquainted,' I replied, for I was still pretty obstinate—the Christian spirit is rather slow to take root, I fear.

There were about ten witnesses to the scene. Ludvík's wife Madla was quite shaken. It was horribly embarrassing, she told me afterwards, but I was completely justified in taking the attitude I did. To throw a man out as Vránek had done by that letter, and then to hold out one's hand to him in public, that was a bit too much.

I played my last game under interesting circumstances. The date was 10 June 1971. Our club chairman had phoned to tell me that a team from Moscow University, which had come to play the Prague students, had suggested having a friendly match during their visit, and they had chosen our club. Somewhat diffidently, the chairman invited me to play—for one thing, my absence would weaken our team against what promised to be fairly strong competition, and also my participation could be interpreted as a gesture of good will in the process of normalizing relations with the Soviet chess players, while it might possibly help my prospects, too. At first, I was afraid that my acceptancy might be misinterpreted, but then I reflected that nobody who knew me would believe that I had recanted. In any case, I had never really broken off my friendly relations with the Soviet chess people. So I agreed to play. I even helped the club by providing a gift—a nicely framed picture of Lenin playing chess with Maxim Gorky—they could give it to our guests without mentioning that it came from me.

And so it was—we played the match in a most friendly atmosphere. My opponent was the young Moscow master, Dubinsky. I went for him, sacrificing rook for a minor piece and avoiding a possible draw. Then he hit on some excellent moves, and with time running out, he was pressing me uncomfortably. But routine is routine, so we ended with a draw. As we said good-bye, I asked the head of the team to convey my warm greetings to my old comrades, Botvinnik and Flohr, which he promised to do.

Two days later, our chairman was on the phone to tell me, with trembling voice, that there was big trouble. It seemed that the Soviet Ambassador had telephoned the Communist Party Central Committee in Prague to say that my participation in the match was a provocation—appropriate steps must be taken immediately. The message had been faithfully handed down to the chairman of ČSTV. Four days after receiving this behest, the executive of that body duly took steps. The two officials who had organized the event—one being the chairman of our club—

were removed from office; I was stripped of my title 'Honoured Master of Sport', and commanded to 'halt all chess activities until the case be fully investigated', on the grounds that I had 'disobeyed the ban on international representation'. Of course, I appealed immediately against this decision, pointing out that the whole thing was absurd because the rules made no provision for 'banning international representation'. Naturally, I also stressed that I had been persuaded to play by the responsible officials, who saw in my agreement an expression of good will.

Nevertheless, on 30 June, the ČSTV executive adopted two resolutions—the first rejecting my appeal, the second expelling me from the organization. So, from that moment, I could not even go to the club for a game of chess. My thirty-three-year career seemed to have been brought to a full stop. To be kicked out like that from the game I had played, for better or for worse, so long—wasn't it a bit much? Yet I knew that others had met with even harsher treatment. I recalled, for instance, the case of our famous gymnast, Vera Čáslavská.

Vera is our most successful sportswoman of all time. How many Olympic gold medals she has won, not to mention other Olympic medals, how many times she has been European and world champion—that I cannot venture to say from memory, but the figures are pretty high. During the Tokyo Olympic Games the newspapers declared that she had done more for her country than dozens of diplomats, and her last appearance at the Mexico Olympics in the autumn of 1968 was again a triumph. One would think that any government must be proud of such a woman. But in June 1968 Vera signed the '2000 Words' and from 1969 onwards innumerable attempts were made to persuade her to show, by withdrawing her signature, that she regretted her action. But Vera felt no regret and she refused to oblige. Consequently, all doors were shut to her, and she was not allowed to accept offers to work abroad as a trainer. The Americans wanted to make a film with her—which would have earned a packet of dollars for Czechoslovakia—but that, too, was banned. When she had completed a book for which she had a contract, it could not be published. Then her husband was thrown out of the Army. And then there were the endless interviews with officials. On one such occasion the chairman of ČSTV demanded that she break off relations with 'unsuitable friends', myself included. Vera replied that she valued our friendship and had no intention of losing it.

One day she was invited to visit the officials in Prague of her sports section, 'Red Star', apparently to discuss her suggestion that she train children since she was barred from working with representatives. The meeting, as she described it to us afterwards, had an air of utter unreality.

Some thirty people were sitting round a table—since Vera recognized only one of them, the committee must have been completely changed. When she entered the room they continued with their business, taking not the slightest notice of her. She stood looking at them until it occurred to somebody to kick a chair in her direction, which she took to be an invitation to be seated. Otherwise they ignored her presence until, in the end, she indicated that she would like to say something. She had been invited to come, she pointed out, but it seemed she was in the way, and since she realized that her membership must be an embarrassment to them, she would like to ease the situation by resigning. At this the chairman leapt to his feet, shouting:

'Did you hear her, comrades? She offers to resign, does she? That beats everything! So she thinks she's the one to decide! Not on your life, comrades! We'll decide! And I move that we expel Comrade Čáslavská. Who's in favour?'

They were all in favour with the exception of the member whom Vera knew from the old committee—he abstained. In a matter of minutes the joint Olympic and World Champion in gymnastics was expelled from Czechoslovak sport. And if this famous sportswoman could suddenly be treated with such discourtesy and brushed aside at will, what did I expect? Why, they had treated me quite courteously, even taking the trouble to go through the motions of official procedure.

I was anxious, none the less, to make a last desperate bid—to part with something resembling the work of a lifetime comes hard when one is still of an age to carry on. So I addressed my third letter to the chairman of the International Chess Federation, Professor Euwe of Amsterdam. I asked the Federation to intervene because I considered my expulsion to have been in contravention of the FIDE rules prohibiting any kind of racial, religious or political discrimination. Indeed, mine was the first instance of a chess player being expelled on political grounds. Moreover, I had taken an active part in FIDE for many years, so from that standpoint, too, my case should not be a matter of indifference.

None of my letters were answered. True, Professor Euwe sent a message by Luboš Kaválek notifying his intention to visit Prague in order to discuss the matter personally with our Federation and myself, but nothing more was heard of this. However, I cannot hold it against FIDE if they were anxious to avoid any unpleasantness with Russia, which has the strongest chess organization in the world.

As a last resort, it occurred to me that I might be able to play chess by correspondence. But when I sent an application to enter a correspondence competition organized in Slovakia, my entry was refused. Then I discovered by chance that the *Bund Deutscher Fernschach-Freunde*, with headquarters in Hamburg, was open to foreign members. Full of hope, I posted my application to Herr von Masow, chairman of the organization. After some delay, the reply came—I could not be admitted to membership, I would understand the reason. I would have preferred them to tell me themselves, then at least I could have argued with them, but there it was.

Finally, I started two games with Mr. Mattheenssen of Kapellan in Belgium, who wrote that he was old, he had played with Lasker and Koltanowski. At last someone was willing to play with me; perhaps we would both get some pleasure from it.

I was occupied in those days with writing a book and taking cures for my various ailments. On the whole the press left me in peace, and I kept quiet. But then journalist Vladimír Škutina was brought to trial. I had made only a passing acquaintance with him in 1969 when we met at two or three meetings, then, in the autumn of the same year, we were both in Pankrác Prison—

apparently he had once seen me marching round the courtyard. Now he had been served with the incredible sentence of fifty months, and we were in close touch with his wife and little daughter. Early in July my friend Jan Vlk—a young man who, having just taken his degree in philosophy, was employed in consequence as a cashier in a restaurant—came to tell me that a representative of a Dutch radio station would like to interview myself, Vlk and Jan Šling about the Škutina case. Jan Vlk was worried; he had not really wanted to ask me, he said, because I was sufficiently at risk already. But I assured him I felt we must do something to help—and to be frank I think I was itching to break my silence.

So the three of us met next day. The Dutchman came with a tape-recorder in a brief-case, and we drove a short distance into the countryside to record the interview. I spoke German, Šling English, because he knew no German, while Vlk spoke in Czech, having no knowledge of either English or German. The significance of this circumstance will appear later.

Both these young men belong to families victimized in the 1950s. Šling's father was the first to be arrested among those Communists later alleged to be members of the 'Slánsky anti-State conspiratorial centre', and he was one of the eleven executed. Vlk's father was sentenced to fifteen years in prison as the alleged leader of a fictitious 'Great Trotskyist Council'. A few months after exposure of the frame-up had secured his release, he died. Now both sons had been addressing protest letters to Dr. Husák about the recurrence of political persecution and trials.

My critical remarks, in a fairly mild statement, were: 'The sentence on Vladimír Škutina is, in my view, harsh and unjust, and I find it impossible to keep silent about it.' And later: 'For many years I have been a dedicated and active Communist. Today I still feel a sense of guilt when I see how Communist parties in countries where they are not in power proclaim slogans about freedom of the press, freedom of assembly and so on, and I compare these sentiments with the fate of civil rights in countries where Communist parties are in power.' Questioned about chess, I faithfully recounted the history of my expulsion, adding one item which I had learned subsequently—namely, that the white-haired gentleman who chaired the commission, Dr. Jiří Kepák by name, had been one of the prosecutors at the trial in 1950 at which Dr. Milada Horáková had been condemned to death—the first time that a show trial in Eastern Europe had resulted in the judicial murder of a woman. Otherwise, I kept a watch on what I said. Vlk was also quite moderate, but Šling made up for it with gusto.

On 2 August the interview was transmitted by Radio Hilversum II, and then the fat was in the fire. Our radio went for me with a will. The first broadside started roughly as follows: 'Once a slim youth filled with ideals, he toured factories and offices setting up chess groups. Later he became a grandmaster of chess—yes, you've guessed whom we're talking about, it's Luděk Pachman.'

The talk went on to explain how, not having had much success in chess, I had sought fame in other fields. I had found my victim in the person of Central Committee member, František Vodsloň, whose speeches I wrote, thereby gaining the opportunity to spread my views at the highest political level. Finally, I had lost the game, and now I was spitting poison on the Party and the Communist movement altogether, as demonstrated by . . . etc.

A follow-up programme repeated the allegation that, with the aid of the media abroad, I was begging for foreign alms. 'And no mean sums are involved,' continued the speaker, giving full rein to his imagination, 'the gifts in the accounts of several prominent persons of that ilk amount in a single year to 11 million dollars.'

When someone quoted this to me, I thought they must have misheard—11,000 would have been pretty good—but no, later I saw the statement in black and white in the Dutch monitor report.

18. Holy Matrimony

■▪■▪■▪■▪■▪■▪■▪■▪■▪■▪■▪■▪■▪■▪■▪■▪■▪■▪■

Eužénie had been learning the catechism and going to church with me. Her baptism was fixed for 5 September, and our church wedding would be the day after on our silver wedding day.

I had envisaged a quiet affair, but the priest told me that the ceremony should be linked, if possible, with the celebration of Holy Mass. So I had fifty invitations printed, which I sent to our friends, who would come to the silver wedding party in the evening. At the top of the card I put the text 'Behold, we count them happy which endure' (James, 5: 11), with a big 25 beneath, meaning we hoped to endure for many years to come. Of course, one could find a double meaning and, to be honest, I have to admit that in the 'Ten Points' petition we had also written that it was necessary to endure.

When I went to confession on Friday, 3 September, I was greeted with bad news. Someone in the Government, probably the Minister for Culture, had told the Bishop that our ceremony would be regarded as a hostile act on the part of the Church. Of course, we were entitled to go ahead, the priest told me, but should we decide not to, the Bishop could declare our marriage in 1946 valid in the eyes of the Church. To this I agreed, but I preferred to postpone confession for a few days until my anger had passed.

Now we had the problem of informing the invited guests about this last-minute cancellation. Since the priest was anxious that I should not make an appearance at the church—as it transpired, he showed great foresight—we decided that my wife should be there at the appointed time to make our apologies to any friends who might turn up. Then we would meet for a late lunch at the Waldstein Inn in Prague's Little Quarter.

Soon after Euženie arrived at the church, a big car drew up near by, and four men jumped out and took up a position opposite the entrance. Then another car appeared, with another four men equipped with a camera and various pieces of apparatus. A third car disgorged a further foursome, who went into a near-by wine restaurant, from which they emerged with glasses of wine to stand gazing in the direction of the church. Meanwhile, two uniformed policemen were patrolling the vicinity.

As our guests started coming, Euženie asked them to leave and, seeing the company we had, they needed little persuasion. Suddenly, a cameraman and his crew appeared—a few days later, *Rudé právo* reported that he was Herr Galeti from a West German television company. Having surveyed the scene, they asked Euženie if this was the church of St. Havel, to which she replied that if they had come for the wedding, it was not taking place. As they were speaking, the men opposite started filming, whereupon Herr Galeti brought his camera into action to film the others. The two uniformed policemen immediately approached him, asking to see his papers and to know what he was doing there. Showing them his press card, he explained that he was filming ancient buildings in Prague, naturally the church of St. Havel interested him. So they let him depart in peace. Soon after this incident, Euženie ended her vigil and precisely at 3.45 p.m. we took our seats in the Waldstein Inn.

The table next to ours was occupied by a gentleman and a young lady. The gentleman listened as unobtrusively as possible over the wood partition separating us. I ordered food for the five of us present, with three pints and two halves of beer, remarking that two of us were drivers. As they had bottled beer only, Euženie and I shared one bottle, and of that we consumed only part. Nevertheless, mindful of our strict regulations concerning drinking and driving, we spun out our meal for an hour.

As we were driving away, a police car stopped us—traffic control, it seemed. When I presented my documents, one of the officers asked where I was employed. On hearing that I was unemployed, he wondered how such a thing was possible. I assured him that I would be grateful for advice about where to find a job, I had tried at least twelve firms without success. Then they fired the question with which they had been primed: 'There's alcohol in your breath, what have you been drinking?'

Naturally, having, as I told them, consumed less than half a pint of beer, I was surprised at this, but I complied with their demand that I take a breath test. They snatched the balloon from my mouth before I could see the result, and announced that they were taking me for a blood test.

So I got into the police car, while the others went home. At the hospital a nurse took a blood sample and a doctor examined me. After the usual tests he announced that I had had nothing worth mentioning and could leave. The police officer, however, thought otherwise, and he put me in a small room to wait. When about half an hour had passed, I demanded to speak with the officer in charge who, in reply to my query why I had to wait, replied: 'Just sit there, you've loads of time.' Patiently I explained that it was my silver wedding day and guests were expecting me at home.

'We've no time to talk with drunken drivers,' he retorted.

I informed him that I could not be classified as a drunken driver until they had the test result, until then they must presume me innocent.

'When we have the result, you'll be a drunken driver,' he declared. To which I replied that in three days, when the result would be known, no driver could still be drunk.

Even my request to use the phone was refused. I was forced to sit in that cubby-hole for a full three hours.

In the meantime, Euženie had been searching for me. When she phoned the police station where I was sitting in quiet meditation, they told her I was not there. She even routed out my one-time interrogator, Lieutenant Cibulka, only to learn that his department had certainly not arrested me.

Back home, she found nineteen guests sitting around, touching neither food nor drink, with their spirits somewhere below freezing point. Finally, with two of the company, she managed to

154

locate me and, when the officer in charge had just summoned me to his presence, she burst into the room with a policeman grabbing at her sleeve. They had told her, apparently, that I was being interrogated, but she argued that since I was not under arrest, she could join me. That she did by bursting like a bombshell from the waiting-room into the inner sanctum.

When, at last, they let us go, the others rejoiced that now we would be able to celebrate.

'Not a bit of it,' said I, 'we're going back to the hospital laboratory.'

I explained that the police had taken the blood sample. Supposing someone had had a good drink at the public expense, and they had substituted the sample for mine? I would have another sample taken. At the hospital they grasped the situation at once. All the doctors and nurses present gathered round as witnesses, and they promised to deliver the blood to the forensic laboratory themselves.

By the time we got home, it was eleven. We had an uproarious welcome, followed by presents. Historian Tesář came up with a truly original gift—a genuine, pre-war general's sword. I had to draw it from the scabbard while we all cried out, 'Faithful unto death!' Travel writer Hanzelka and his wife gave us a kitten, and when I asked people to suggest a name, someone said, 'Why, Ucho, of course!' and all with one voice proclaimed 'Ucho!'

I should explain that Ucho is an abbreviation originating from one of our meetings on Rowers Island. Someone remarked that we could almost describe ourselves as a Centre for Czechoslovak Resistance (the initial letters in Czech are UČO, phonetically, Ucho), so I said: 'That's fine, we can call ourselves Ucho when we're arranging meetings over the phone, that'll give them something to puzzle over.' So the kitten was duly christened.

On the Wednesday after the party I got busy with applying for a pension. It was no simple matter. I had been on the sick list until the middle of May, then I needed a job—not because I had not sufficient work to do at home, but I might run into trouble with the authorities if I seemed to be idle (we have a law about 'parasites'). None of the vacancies offered to me by the labour department of the local council had yielded any result—everywhere I had been fobbed off with some excuse. Then they decided I would have to do manual work, but for that the doctors declared me unfit. Now, after further medical check-ups, I was called before a commission which would decide about a pension. They awarded me a modest partial disability pension.

The next morning, having somehow earned the luxury of being given the newspapers in bed, I read on the second page of *Rudé právo* the following headline: '666 words about a mishap—even a grandmaster can blunder'. At some length in would-be sarcastic vein, liberally sprinkled with attempts at an analogy with chess, the writer described the events of our wedding anniversary, not omitting scathing reference to beer-drinking and the action by the police—the implication being, of course, that I had been guilty of drunken driving.

I jumped out of bed and got down to work. First, I established two facts—the name appended to the article was not that of anyone on the *Rudé právo* staff; second, the Waldstein Inn is a wine restaurant where they serve only one beer per head with a main dish—the manager would testify to this in writing and give evidence in court if necessary. Then I went to get the result of the blood test. Interestingly enough, it seemed to have disappeared, so I asked for a duplicate. With some hesitation, the laboratory agreed, and the result was clear—o per cent of alcohol in the blood, and the official test gave the same result.

I took a taxi, since my driving licence was still in the hands of the police. The driver, I noticed, left his meter off, but I made no comment—if he wanted to fleece me, let him. When he drew up, I asked how much I owed, to which he replied: 'Don't be offended, Mr. Pachman, but I would like to give you the journey as a token of my respect.'

I wondered how he knew me, but he made me feel a lot better.

In the afternoon as I was drafting a statement for *Rudé právo*, a commentary came over on the radio, repeating the substance of the newspaper story, including the bit about the beer-drinking and the confiscation of my driving licence. Subsequent inquiries showed that the speaker's name was unknown in Czechoslovak

Radio—so now not only the nightmare voices over the telephone, but journalists, too, were assuming non-existent, but fine-sounding Czech names.

Naturally, I received no satisfaction from any of the official quarters to which I wrote in connection with this affair. But from Dr. Thomášek, Bishop of Prague and Papal Administrator, I received a certificate recognising our civil wedding in 1946 as valid from the start in the eyes of the Church. The council official who performed the ceremony cannot have known that he was playing the part of a priest! Shortly after, our marriage promise was confirmed at St. Havel's where we were one among about fifty married couples. I sent a full report on the whole matter to the Bishop, telling him that I was suing *Rudé právo* and Czechoslovak Radio. In reply I received a very kind letter, beginning with the words 'Dear Friend', and blessing us both.

19. Milan and Jana

When I returned home from prison in December 1970, we planned to invite a child from a children's home to spend Christmas with us. On visiting an institution near Prague, I found that a seven-year-old gipsy boy would be available. We had to cancel the visit, however, because I was still unwell and my mother-in-law also fell ill, while my wife had to go to work between Christmas and the New Year, so it would be impossible to give the boy proper attention.

Then, in the autumn of 1971, I visited the home in good time, towards the end of October. I had to inform the head that since I was a 'dismissed journalist', we were unlikely to obtain permission to adopt a child, but we could, at least, offer a temporary home to one of her charges.

Having written 'dismissed journalist', I realize that some explanation is due. In December 1970 my friends had told me of their experiences with the commission appointed by the Journalists Union to purge its ranks. Some had refused the summons to attend, contending that the union leadership was illegal, it had not been elected and, to make matters worse, it was composed of people who had never written for the press. Ludvík, however, attended. He faced the five- to six-member commission with his coat on. When one of them invited him to take it off, he replied, 'That won't be necessary, I'll just stand in my coat.'

Surprise all round. Did he think it would be over so quickly, they said, pointing meaningfully to the fat file on the table.

'You're much mistaken, gentlemen,' Ludvík said, 'we'll be finished immediately. I have come to tell you two things. First you addressed me in your letter as Comrade Vaculík; kindly note that I am not your comrade, I am Mr. Vaculík. Second, you forgot to write in conclusion, "with respects", so please remember next time.'

He departed, and next day the papers reported that L. Vaculík had been expelled from the Journalists Union on account of various 'anti' activities.

For my part, when I received no summons to appear before the commission after my return from prison, I felt a bit anxious. Was I to be left out? In January I visited the union offices to pay my dues, and I still felt myself to be a journalist. Then in June, hearing that there was to be a meeting of free-lance journalists (i.e. those not working—for an employer—one could hardly say they were 'free'), I expected an invitation to attend. When none came, I wrote to ask if there had been some mistake. The reply indicated that I had been expelled on 20 December, I suppose the case seemed so clear that my presence was not required.

Returning now to our plan to enlarge our family over Christmas: early in November I had arranged to fetch the newcomer for a preliminary visit. A few days before the appointed day, however, came the news that Dr. Tesář, the historian who had already been in prison in connection with the 'Ten Points', had been arrested together with several members of the Evangelical Church—a minister, a choirmaster, a professor of philosophy and one other. I had not known that Tesář was a member of this church, he had never mentioned it to me. The news upset me the more because many of my friends belonged to the denomination. I had even considered joining them as there seemed less ostentation about their services, but then I thought better of it. 'There shall be one fold and one shepherd'—but we have about six Evangelical Churches. Since they have no faith in the Papists, why cannot they agree among themselves? I said as much to my friends, but we remained friends, none the less.

Now our plans had to be changed again. I decided to visit Mrs. Tesář—she would be in trouble with three children to care for. When I had driven a short distance, however, the sight of two, possibly three cars following me induced me to change course. So this was it—perhaps they thought I was an Evangelical, too, although *Rudé právo* had written about my religious affiliation

159

and surely Security men ought to read the Party paper! At first I determined, just for the fun of it, to try to shake off my shadows. But after playing hide-and-seek for a while, it occurred to me that this was nonsense, it could be more entertaining to let them follow me. I drove to the Central Army Club, where the three cars hastily looked for parking space near me. Entering the building, I spoke to the porter, and soon two officers in uniform came out to my car with a bulky parcel. Alarm was evident in the Volga, the car nearest to mine. Two of the crew jumped out and strode to the porter's desk while I drove off with all three vehicles in pursuit.

My destination was the Vaculík home. As I approached the house with the parcel in my arms, one of the crew followed me quite openly, obviously deeply suspicious of my errand. The bulky parcel, however, contained an aquarium belonging to a woman who had just been dismissed on political grounds from her employment at the Central Army Club. She had sent a message by Ludvík asking me to collect her property for her. The tough-looking character entered the lift with me, so I asked him politely, 'Which floor?'

'The same as you,' he grunted, whereupon I pressed the button for the third floor, although Ludvík lives on the fifth. On the way up, I engaged him in conversation. One should shadow unobtrusively, I told him, he might get some tips by going to see detective films. I also said that I had no idea what he earned, but however low the pay, it was wasted on him. At that the fellow started swearing—evidently he lacked self-control. He must have been quite low ranking for I have noticed that the higher ranks of his profession keep a better grip on themselves, they try to talk intelligently and, in exceptional cases, they may succeed in that.

On the third floor, I opened the lift door, saying: 'Here we are.' He stepped out while I made a quick move to shut the door and press the button, but—bang!—he landed heavily against the back wall, so we proceeded up together. No blows fell, but for safety's sake I refrained from further conversation. When I rang at the Vaculík's door, the man was standing about two paces behind me. As it happened, both Ludvík and Madla appeared.

'Look at this fellow,' I said to them, 'he's been following me all day and he's bungled the job all the time.'

Ludvík turned to him: 'What do you think you are, man? In any decent country they don't let people know they're being shadowed. If you can't do it, stay at home, it's sheer impudence on your part.'

The man could stand it no longer, he started yelling that he'd fix us all, but when Ludvík stepped threateningly towards him, he turned tail, obviously feeling he was outnumbered by three to one.

A quarter of an hour later, we went downstairs. The Volga had been replaced by a black Tatra, the official limousine which Ludvík calls 'the class enemy'. He finds Volgas more tolerable, even the black ones. With the class enemy following us at a distance of two or three yards and the other cars spaced out behind, I tried the simple trick of crossing traffic lights on the yellow, but our pursuers calmly shot over the red. Finally, Ludvík offered to carry the aquarium himself. There was no point in taking the whole procession to our destination. When I stopped to drop him by a tram stop, one of the crew from the class enemy got out to accompany him while the three cars followed me home. They parked in our street, and once more we were surrounded.

Ludvík telephoned later to tell me about his trip. His companion had waited outside while he delivered the aquarium, then they mounted an almost empty tramcar together. The man thoughtfully seated himself on the opposite side. Soon Ludvík crossed over to sit beside him, and, in a friendly tone, remarked: 'Yours is a tough job, isn't it?' 'Yes,' agreed the man, 'people think it's money for jam, but it isn't.' This encouraged Ludvík to suggest that they might save time by sharing a taxi. His companion welcomed the idea, but said he would need a receipt for the fare. Then, having agreed on that point, they conversed in a friendly manner on the drive into town.

The situation prompted me to address yet another complaint to the Ministry of the Interior. I mentioned that I felt myself physically threatened by cars following close on my tail and, in total disregard of traffic regulations, crossing lights on the red. Moreover, our neighbours were alarmed by what was going on— therefore this was a case of physical intimidation. I received no reply.

A young neighbour came to tell me what had happened to him. Coming home late, he saw three men sitting on a bench in the garden of his house. When he asked them what they were doing there, they told him to bugger off if he didn't want his nose punched.

Nor was I the only victim of harassment in those days. The nuclear physicist, Professor Janouch, was shadowed and pestered by attempts to search his car. And my friend, Karel Kyncl, came off badly. He had chosen the same manoeuvre at crossroads as I had done, managing, so he told me, to drive exactly according to the regulations, with the police almost without exception shooting the lights on the red. Nevertheless, two uniformed policemen visited him at his place of work to confiscate his driving licence because he ignored the lights.

When next day our house was still surrounded, I telephoned Dr. Zahora, former chairman of our Party branch, asking him to accompany me to the Prosecutor's office. As luck would have it, at the first crossroads on our drive there, the class enemy nearly crashed me from the rear. We reported everything, a record was made, with Dr. Zahora and the Vaculíks entered as witnesses. By the afternoon the watchers had been withdrawn from our street. Chance? Or had they discovered I was not a member of the Evangelical Church? Or did the Prosecutor's office still carry some weight?

That Friday evening was, after all, a festive occasion in our family. My wife brought ten-year-old Milan from the children's home for his first visit. After supper we played games, then he told us his story. His father had deserted the family when Milan was three, his mother had been missing for two years. When we learnt that he had an elder sister, Jana, in the home we resolved that her twelfth birthday, a week later, would be celebrated with us and that for Christmas and all future visits they would come together.

Next day I took the boy round Prague. We went into the maze, I told him about the Battle of Lipany and, on Charles Bridge, about the battle against the Swedes. He found it hard to believe that the war had lasted for thirty years and ended in the very middle of the bridge. Then we visited the park, where we found a host of attractions. By midday I had had just about enough, but there was still the zoo. I gave up by the lions, leaving Euženie to complete the tour. The programme on Sunday was just as full. On our arrival at the children's home in the evening, about ten youngsters crowded round us, while Jana stood aloof looking sad. Euženie hugged her and told her she would be spending her birthday with us.

On Christmas Eve Jana decorated the tree and Milan helped me bake Christmas loaves, eating raisins while we worked. This was my first real achievement in cooking since my scouting days. Then came the excitement of presents. No one wanted to go to bed, and in the end the children went with us to midnight mass at St. Wenceslas Church, which was packed so that we only just managed to get in.

We also took the children to the cinema several times, after which there were debates. Having seen a western, Milan was full of theories about how to defend a fortress. But the biggest discussion was over a Romanian film about freedom fights against the Turks. Milan was annoyed that our King Rudolph II had not helped the Romanian prince, that he had pretended to be his friend, then stabbed him in the back. I explained that princes and emperors are like that, that is how it goes in the world, but he declared that if someone were his friend, he would never desert him.

We arranged with the home that the children would visit us again in a fortnight, but that was not to be.

20. Interrogation

An event which I have left out of my story so far is the election of November 1971. There is really little I can say, because what I know is mostly hearsay. We avoided taking any part. When a canvasser visited us a week before polling day, he turned out to be a decent man who was not shocked when we told him we had no intention of voting. The remainder of his visit was spent in discussing cybernetics.

The polls were open for two days—with, of course, just the one official list of candidates to vote for. On the second day, a lady from our street rang our bell in great agitation. When our mother opened the door, the lady begged us not to be angry, she and her family were going to vote because everyone else was going. I wondered why she came to tell us, we had spoken to no one about the elections. And why should we be angry?

Several friends telephoned to tell us that members of the election commission had visited them with a ballot box, suggesting that perhaps they had forgotten to vote. I was sorry that no one had come to us. I had prepared refreshments for them. Evidently our votes were not wanted.

Of the anecdotes told me by friends after the event, I will mention just two. A former chief editor, now a rooftiler, received two canvassers with surprise—elections, did they say? He had heard nothing about that, he was a worker and was not interested in politics. Evidently having no idea who he was, the visitors at once asked with great friendliness if they might step inside. They were at pains to explain to our friend that the working class was now the ruling class and he, as a worker, should exercise his rights.

'But I don't want to rule, I'm a tiler, so my job is to tile roofs.'

164

Ah, but if the working class stopped ruling, they said, the capitalists would come back. He was surprised at that, where would they come from? From the imperialist West, it seemed. Then he asked what parties one could vote for, to which they replied that there were not any parties, there was a single list of candidates.

'Then why should I vote? It's obvious beforehand who'll be elected, so I'd rather stay at home and do some gardening.'

That, they said, would be wrong, one should vote in order to show one's support for socialism. When he asked who was the candidate for their constituency, they proudly announced that, for the Federal Parliament, he was Dr. Gustav Husák.

'Husák?' said our friend. 'Isn't he the rather stout one who often talks on television? He doesn't look much good.'

'Comrade, it's not a beauty competition, it's a matter of who is a good politician. You'll know our candidate for the City Council, he lives in this street—Comrade . . .'

'What, that fellow? Why, in '68 he was spouting about democracy and reform, now he talks quite differently. In that case, I certainly shan't vote.'

Greatly embarrassed, they suggested coming again when he had had time to think it over. And they came—with glum faces, handing him his polling card without comment. They must have found out who he was.

Some friends of ours had a son who was just about to take his school-leaving examination. Although the parents were not going to vote, it was decided that the boy should. He could do what he liked with his ballot paper, but go to the polls he must, otherwise he would be reported at school and probably not be allowed to sit the examination. Unwillingly, he agreed and, with another boy who had the same problem, he went to the polling station. On the way in, a gentleman handed them a card signed by the Mayor of Prague, who thanked them for coming to vote for the first time and told them something about socialism. So the lads decided not to bother about going behind the screen—in any case, everything one did was perfectly visible. Into the envelope intended for the ballot paper they placed the Mayor's message, and the ballot papers they shoved into their pockets as souvenirs.

An official rushed up to them, asking: 'What was that you put in the ballot box?'

'Why, that paper you gave us, weren't we supposed to?'

The official lamented, they were meant to keep it as a memento, and had they put in their ballot papers? They assured him they had, at which he calmed down and gave them the Mayor's message again.

My friend's son went home and, without saying anything, he pinned up that message in their domestic exhibition of similar trophies—in the lavatory. There, carefully framed, hung three awards for building socialism, a prize for journalism and a military award. When the father discovered the addition, a box on the ears threatened. The son considered this unjust. When, two months later, a police search was made in their home, the horrified officers summoned a photographer to record the exhibition, with all the documents as well as evidence of where they were situated. An hour spent struggling with the camera, sitting, standing, lying down, failed to get the scene into one shot and, in the father's subsequent indictment, there was no mention of this lavatory after all.

On Friday, 7 January, the Associated Press correspondent, Mr. Kramer, came to see me. I had once given him a brief interview about my return to the Church, and he had also written about the drunken driving affair. Now he had come to say good-bye, because he was leaving Czechoslovakia. He would like to do one more interview. I was not keen, for what could I say—play the prophet, or talk about sticking it out? Anyhow, no one was particularly interested in us any more, what did it matter whether Dubček or Husák was in power? Mr. Kramer said it did matter, but it was true that interest was waning, that was why AP was transferring him to West Germany. Finally, we agreed to talk not about politics, but about the coming match between Fischer and Spassky—that was what I was really qualified to talk about. I would put it on paper, asking myself the questions because he knew little about chess.

He said that a marvellous close to his stint in Prague would be an interview with Josef Smrkovský. I thought, yes, that would be fine for you, but what if Smrkovský has to take the rap? Aloud, I said he had spoken only once since 1969 for an Italian Communist paper. I doubted whether he would be willing to do anything for AP. However, Mr. Kramer jotted down five questions and asked me to try to arrange something.

On Saturday we visited the Kyncls, where I mentioned the matter. Since Karel and I had agreed that on the Monday I would pick him up at the hospital where he worked, we decided we would take the opportunity of going to see Smrkovský on our way home.

It was Monday morning before I looked at Kramer's notes. On reading the last question: 'Mr. Smrkovský, in our country it is said that you were the Czech politician who, in May 1945, prevented the American Army from liberating Prague. If that is true, what is your opinion about it today?' I put the paper aside impatiently. I certainly had no intention of showing that to Smrkovský. Every child knows the story of how, at Yalta, Churchill wrote a list of European countries with percentages against them showing the proposed balance of East and West influence. Stalin took the list, nodded approvingly, laughed—and the fate of Eastern Europe was decided. But Stalin did not take the plan too seriously. In our country, for instance, it was to have been fifty-fifty, but in 1948 he tipped the balance, with the help of his faithful followers, including myself and most of my friends, to a hundred to nil. If Smrkovský had somehow got in the way of the Yalta plan, what was he to say? That he was a Communist, therefore he wanted the liberation to be a working-class affair? I left the notes at home and changed the programme—I would take Karel straight to our place.

It was precisely 2.29 p.m.—I dislike unpunctuality—when I parked by the hospital. The space ahead of me was occupied by a Volga. As I got out of my car, two men jumped out of the car in front. One took me by the right arm, the other by the left, and the first man said tenderly: 'Mr. Pachman, you're coming with us, we need to talk to you.'

I demanded to know what they wanted to talk about, but they said I would find out later. I would also see a warrant later, it seemed. In the meantime the first officer waved a card under my nose, saying his name was Captain Maxa, he had conducted the search of our place in August 1969. So, old friends!

They took me to headquarters in Bartolomějská Street, where I was expected—they would first search my person. Referring to the relevant article of the law, I demanded their warrant, but they simply caught hold of me and turned my pockets inside out. Apparently they failed to find what they were looking for. But they laughed on finding in my wallet two pictures I had bought from an invalid outside St. Wenceslas Church. In the list of belongings I later read: 'two sacred pictures'. Then two of the officers left, while the third sat down to engage me in conversation. Since I had all these foreign contacts, I might write about him for the Western press, he suggested. 'Which of the correspondents do you know among the Americans, for instance?'

I told him I knew lots of correspondents, best of all that Dutch 'spy', Verkijk. He was not interested in Verkijk, he shrugged off the 'spy' bit, but what about Americans?

Replying that I knew plenty of Americans, too, I was at the same time rapidly reviewing in my mind how they could know about Mr. Kramer's visit. Karel would never have said a word, and I had not mentioned it to anyone else. There was just one explanation—bugging of our place or the Kyncls'. But no, not ours, it had to be the Kyncls'—we had arranged there about meeting at the hospital, and the Volga was obviously lying in wait. At a much later date, I learnt that at 2.30 p.m. precisely Karel was nabbed on his way out to meet me.

Also much later I heard that a house search had already been in progress at home while we were being arrested. The law provides that a search can be made if there are grounds for suspecting that an article pertaining to a criminal charge may be present on the premises. A warrant has to be issued, the accused is to be interrogated and given the opportunity to tell the authorities where the articles concerned are to be found. Of course, I had not been interrogated before the search, in fact, charges had not even been laid. They chose the opposite course—first search and then frame the charges. In the event that nothing material was found, they had a 'reserve charge', which also materialized in my case.

Euženie knows all about house searches. She demanded a warrant in writing, which caused much telephoning to headquarters. Then she required the presence of an independent witness as laid down in the Code. After some argument, they allowed her to call Dr. Zahora. Until he came and throughout the preliminary exchanges, she would not let the officers sit down, so they stood obediently at attention for over an hour.

Then came a ring at the bell—the Hanzelkas had been invited to come and see how the kitten, Ucho, was getting on. Accompanied by the officer in command, Euženie opened the door and, before he could stop her, she said straight out what was happening. The Hanzelkas hurried away to spread the news that I was in trouble again.

My wife's determined behaviour upset the authorities. My interrogator told me later that she had a very bad influence on me.

When Dr. Zahora arrived, the search could start. They soon found the Kramer notes on my desk and one of them took them away at once. Among other things confiscated were two typewriters and a mass of documents, including a chapter of my memoirs entitled 'Quiet Time', describing my life since December 1970—I had thought it would be a quiet time! They also took the letter from the Bishop. When I wrote subsequently requesting its return, they refused on the grounds that it could be regarded as condoning a criminal offence. That distressed me so much that I wrote to the Bishop. In his reply he said: 'My son, it doesn't matter at all, I condone no offence and to give a blessing is not forbidden.'

While the five-hour search was in progress I was waiting at police headquarters. When some hours had passed, they took me across the street to a building labelled 'Federal Ministry of the Interior, Investigation Section, State Security'—I had been promoted. There they sat me down by a typewriter, saying they would write a statement. When I demanded charges in writing they said I had not even been detained yet, merely summoned to appear. That being the case, I decided to go ahead without a lawyer (supposing they found they had drawn a blank, and let me go?).

We talked about the Dutch radio interview. That they had let the matter lie for six months, then picked me up in a hurry in the street, seemed odd to say the least. Evidently it was a pretext, and they were after something else. Anyhow, I was quite happy to talk about the Hilversum affair—it was trivial enough and the whole thing was recorded, so why question me about it?

In the middle of the interrogation, a man burst in triumphantly waving the Kramer notes. Now we would really talk, he announced. That was no surprise to me after all those questions about American journalists and, in any case, there was no point in concealing Kramer's name. It would be a scoop if they started chasing Kramer, while the most they could do was to deport him. Which meant that I should tell all. With great pleasure I dictated my statement, putting on record that Smrkovský knew nothing about the proposed interview. I had decided not to visit him— the proof of which was the notes lying on the table.

Obviously disappointed at drawing a blank, they tried again: 'Did Mr. Kyncl know about this?'

Why should he, I replied, I was not even sure if he knew Smrkovský (that *I* did, they already knew from their files). Again, they were disappointed. When some months later I went to confession, I asked the priest whether it was a sin to lie to the Security police. He told me it was, it is permissible only to keep silent. Inquiring about my reason for lying, he considered the matter and concluded that the sin was not grave. It is, to this day, the only sin I have been unable to regret. But since then I have found it better to be silent than to lie.

At around one o'clock in the morning I was served with charges of incitement and damaging the interests of the Republic abroad. There was no mention of Kramer and Smrkovský. Incitement there was, to my feelings, because the charge sheet included two strong statements which I had never made. I recalled that Šling had made them in the radio interview. Since they can hardly have confused my German with his English, they had probably needed the 'evidence' to justify taking me into custody. I lodged a complaint about this and about the inclusion of statements by myself which in no way constituted a criminal offence. Furthermore, I was at a loss to know why I had been arrested suddenly on the street in connection with a broadcast transmitted in August, whereas it was now January.

On the fourth day I was transferred to Ruzyň. About twenty of us were chained together in two rows, facing each other in a bus. A prisoner opposite me was gazing firmly in my direction. When I saw him, he laughed and shrugged his shoulders as if to say: 'Well, this is it!' When the bus started rattling and the guard was looking out of the window, this prisoner whispered: 'I don't know a thing about Smrkovský, you get it?'

I replied in the tone of Piggy's messages at Ruzyň: 'I get it!', but I forgot to add, 'old cock!'

21. Back Inside

On arrival at Ruzyň I was put in the basement as before. During the first week I went out for exercise once or twice, then I fell ill with my old trouble. Although they gave me a purgative when I asked for it, the tablets had no effect, so I stopped eating. Since the governor had summoned me when I was admitted in order to tell me that to go on hunger strike would be regarded as a breach of discipline, for which I would be punished, I now accepted the meals, only to flush them down the toilet. At least it was something to do, otherwise there was nothing, no books, no writing, just gazing into space.

The inactivity was probably the cause of my further troubles. At night I felt I was suffocating. The sensation was reminiscent of that night in Bohnice, and I tried breathing exercises as a cure. Then I had other strange sensations and ideas. Moreover, although at home I had been thinking I was almost a Christian, I was now incapable of praying properly. I had a recurrence of an idea I had experienced in 1970, a feeling that I had already lived one life as a criminal, a murderer or something of the kind. Now I had been given an opportunity to repent, but again I had failed because I was sinful and selfish, with no proper love for my fellow beings except, perhaps, for Euženie. Suddenly I began thinking about my brother, with whom relations had been strained for some time. Now, sitting in that cell, I decided to write him a letter. I begged his forgiveness—he had been right when he said after August 1968 that I had done nothing but talk and put on airs; it really did make me feel good when people listened to me. I had behaved shockingly to our aunts, and why had it not occurred to me to ask him, too, if he had all he needed. Instead of giving parties in American style, I should have thought

172

of others. All this I wrote, without pausing to think whether the censors would read it. Fortunately, as it transpired later, I did mention that my views on August 1968 were unchanged.

Whether I was still in the cell, or in the sick bay when I wrote, that I cannot recall, but my transfer was the consequence of the following events.

My mind being full of thoughts like those I have described, I came to believe more and more that I had no right to live. Since I had ruined my life by selfishness, perhaps my only absolution lay in death. I had a vague idea that by dying I might save something—my thoughts turned to Jan Palach and similar ideas.

One day my two cell-mates went for exercise while I stayed as usual in the cell. Soon after they left I stood on the table and jumped head first to the floor. My head struck the wooden toilet lid (later, I was charged the sum of 105 crowns for breaking it), then someone was dragging me—I know for certain I was dragged, not carried—along the floor. I came to a bit when the cuts on my forehead and nose were being stitched. Then, firmly strapped to a stretcher, I was taken back to the cell and left on the floor. I must have lain there for two or three days before they transferred me to the sick bay. The other occupant talked a lot about our bishops, from which I judged that he was a stool-pigeon, so I decided not to speak.

The interrogators started visiting me. On the first occasion, I avoided answering questions by saying I felt very ill. Dr. Basch, Chairman of the Czech Chess Federation, was present in his capacity as court interpreter, and I had the impression that he was looking very sadly at me. On the second occasion I agreed to answer questions in writing. The things they asked about seemed absurd: for instance, how far from my mouth had I held the microphone when recording the radio interview. They explained that they needed exact information because they had a tape-recording, which they played over to me while Dr. Basch confirmed that it agreed with the translation on the file—a matter which I had, in any case, affirmed long before.

And now I am going to describe something which, when she

reads it, Eužerne will want me to delete, because she fears people will say I was completely mad at the time. But I have decided to record everything about which I am certain, and about this I am more than certain. Moreover, in the space of three years, eleven psychiatrists concluded that I was not mad, in consequence of which it was impossible for them to put me away in Bohnice (presumably they couldn't find a twelfth man for the job).

I was in a bad way at the time; three nights running I felt completely suffocated. On the third night, I suddenly sat up in bed with the fixed idea that God wished me to die. But I was afraid, and I begged God to forgive me for not wishing to obey His will. Then I recalled that in 1970 I had found among the books sent from home a copy of Seneca's letters to Lucretius, in which he writes that, given sufficient courage and inventiveness, a prisoner can always escape his gaolers by suicide. That seemed to me to be some kind of sign.

The bed appeared very high, the floor of smooth stone. While postponing the decision, I still felt that it had to happen that night. When the morning bell rang and my cellmate was shuffling towards the toilet, I stood on the bed and dived head first to the floor. The impact was slight and to my surprise, I felt no pain. I just stayed half sitting on the floor, while my companion called the warder and told him—evidently he believed it—that I had hit my head on the bed.

They threw me on the bed, tied me down firmly, all of them including my fellow prisoner, behaving very roughly. Occasionally someone stuck a dish of food under my nose, asking if I intended to eat or not, and when I refused there were various rude remarks. I am not sure how many days passed before I was transferred to the Pankrác Prison hospital where, once they started giving me treatment, I soon felt much better. On condition that they would treat my intestinal trouble, too, I decided to end the hunger strike. At that, miracles started to happen—in the morning a lady in a white coat would come to ask how I felt and to tell me my menu for the day. And the food was superb. I could never eat more than half, the rest I gave to the orderly.

After two or three visits from the interrogators and my lawyer, around 10 April the documents in the case were completed. I discovered that they contained trivialities, nothing more than the statements already mentioned, which could not have incited anyone unless he happened to be an exceptionally peppery character. And the reference from my former place of work astounded me. In contrast to the wide-ranging condemnation issued on a previous occasion, this statement referred solely to the period when I had been a member of the editorial staff: I had shown praiseworthy initiative, I was politically and professionally mature, I was popular among my colleagues. The signature was the same as it had been in 1970. Six weeks later I was to learn how it had happened. New regulations, it seemed, now required that such references be discussed by the trade union branch. The chief had read out a piece drafted on the previous lines, but my former colleagues had unexpectedly rebelled, especially one friend of mine. There was no truth in it, he protested, and why write about 1968-9 when I had already left the staff? In short, they displayed a courageous public spirit which didn't prove futile, showing that something can be achieved even against the odds when people stand out for the truth.

The case being closed, I was, of course, put on normal prison food again—the special treatment had lasted about ten days. Then, quite unexpectedly, Euženie appeared. We were allowed to talk for an hour, even to hold hands. She told me that few of our friends were at home—the reason was obvious to me. The prosecutor sitting in on the visit fidgeted in his chair, but he let us talk on. She also gave me a shattering piece of news: my brother had sent copies of that letter of mine to several leading dissidents, including Smrkovský and Vaculík, accompanying it with a reproachful covering letter. He had also sent copies to the press. I was stunned. It had been a purely personal letter, written when I was in a bad way mentally and physically—what caused him to do such a thing?

Euženie left me a parcel containing, among other things, some chess journals, writing paper and three books—the New Testament, Thomas à Kempis's *Imitatio Christi* and Quoist's *Between Man and God*. The last was a present from Emil Zátopek at our last meeting—'Look, somebody's given me a book,' he said, 'it's about God, so it's no use to me, it's more suitable for you.'

First I made a thorough study of the New Testament, making careful notes. Then I tried to make a synthesis of the other two books, searching for an answer to the question: 'How should one live?' Being a Christian, I discovered, is a hard job.

My brother came and they let us talk alone. When I asked why he had circulated my letter, he said he had wanted to help, and that was the best way. I could not agree, but probably he meant well although he could have done me considerable harm. Later I learnt that editors had been told at the last minute not to publish the letter.

Another visitor was the chief interrogator, who came to inform me officially that I would soon be coming to trial, and providing I conducted myself sensibly in court, my case would be judged leniently—no one, it seemed, wanted to persecute me. This surprised me a lot and, I must admit, pleased me.

Once when about to write a letter home, I took an envelope from the middle of the packet, whereupon a slip of paper fell out. It turned out to be the only message my wife had smuggled in during my two terms in prison. The few lines were signed with the initials of a priest whom I knew. My attention was riveted by the following words:

'Should Truth demand the sacrifice of life, it is right, indeed necessary, to give it. Should that not be so, it is wrong, indeed sacrilegious, to insist on giving it. Probably the Lord was not pleased with the external activity, He preferred to see a going out into the wilderness. After his conversion, St. Paul spent three years there.'

It was as if the writer had known all my questions and my doubts. Now I was resolved. I needed to take my synthesis of Thomas à Kempis and Quoist a bit further in the direction of the former. Again I set down ten points, this time not about politics. These were the principles by which I wished to live. And at my trial, I decided, I would take a moderate stand. I needed to get out of prison, where I could find no wilderness. Were I to deliver political speeches in court, I would be preaching to the Security men and my wife, for the public would not be admitted. To my wife I could give the lecture at any time, and it was presumably pointless to imagine I could move the others.

On his next visit the interrogator told me he bore good news. The trial was to be held within a week. I would be tried on all charges—the 'Ten Points', the original charge dating from 1969, and the Radio Hilversum interview. Providing I showed moderation in court, the sentence might not exceed by many months the sum of my two periods of detention. But I must promise not to make public statements or to engage in political activity and, above all, I must not give interviews for publication abroad. I must also tell the court that I was willing to withdraw the civil suit against *Rudé právo* and the radio. On these conditions, I would be released after the trial on health grounds, and I could apply for the remainder of my sentence to be waived.

This I found acceptable, for it was fully in line with my plans for life at home. Paul had no quarrel with the media when he went into the wilderness, nor did he engage in political activity. So I would have to master my conceit.

While agreeing on these conditions to speak as suggested, I insisted that there would be no breast-beating or admission that I had sinned. I would defend myself against the charges. And that, they indicated, would be in order.

My brother came to see me the day before the trial. His advice was that I should disassociate myself in court from the campaign unleashed in the West, where my case was being used to attack our country. The news that there was some kind of campaign pleased me, but I told my brother that I could not disassociate myself from something about which I knew nothing. When he had left I consulted my lawyer. We decided that he would leave the political matters to me, concentrating his defence on the legal aspects.

22. The Verdict

On Thursday, 4 May 1972, I was transported by car to the City Law Courts. The three warders in attendance informed me on the way that I must behave respectfully in court and always stand up when told to do so.

As we drove into the street where the courts are situated, I saw Karel Kyncl's wife running to catch up with us, but the car turned quickly into a back entrance, and we got out in a court-yard. They put me in a basement cell, saying they would fetch me later.

Soon the warders returned, and one chained me with a hand-cuff and led me upstairs. As we were going along a corridor, I heard cries of 'Hullo, Luděk!' Among friends gathered there I saw František Vodsloň, then there were others round the entrance, among them Ludvík with a terrible beard and, above all, Euženie who had managed to get to the front though the guards soon ordered her away.

The court room was tiny—three rows of benches behind me, a long table in front. When Euženie made for the bench nearest me she was immediately told to move back. Other seats were occupied by Security men, court officials and journalists—only two of them—leaving little room for the public. Most of our friends had to stay outside.

First came the reading of the indictment. Euženie took it down in shorthand, after which the presiding judge announced that 'the public is forbidden to take notes', a ban applying solely to my wife, because the journalists were not deterred. Then the presiding judge—the Bench included three more men and one woman—asked me if I felt myself to be guilty. I replied that I
178

had given the true facts during interrogation, I would speak on the matter of guilt in conclusion.

Then the prosecutor came forward with the surprising proposal that the charges dating from 1969—referring mainly to 'defaming' Dr. Husák and my article in *Het Parool*—be taken at a later date. After brief consultation with defence counsel, I agreed. That this was a wise course was proved within a few weeks when the 1969 charges were dropped.

On taking the stand, I was rather put out to find that instead of being taken step by step through the points at issue, I had to make a straight statement. Speaking spontaneously, I said that I took full political responsibility for the 'Ten Points' and the radio interview, but I was not aware of having committed an offence— the 'Ten Points' petition had not been circulated to the public, and in the interview I had stated my views in fairly moderate terms, and moreover, what I said was demonstrably true. I was then questioned.

It soon emerged that the main charge referred to the 'Ten Points', whereas the interview was of no significance. The prosecution picked especially on the scene round the camp fire where I was alleged to have read out the document. By the time the counsel for the defence had finished his questioning, I felt sure the prosecution would have a hard job to make out a case under any article of the Criminal Code.

Then six psychiatrists and psychologists gave it as their opinion that I was mentally normal. Under stress I had suffered profound depression, and continued detention could have a most unfavourable effect on my condition. In the summer of 1971, as an aftermath of the detention psychosis caused by my first term of imprisonment, I had experienced a reduction in my powers of control, but my perceptive capacity was unaffected. They therefore proposed that extenuating circumstances under Article 32 be taken into account.

I wondered about the powers of control—who could help being angry about the treatment of Škutina? But I held my peace, realizing that their line of argument could help me.

In the afternoon three prosecution witnesses were called,

among them Emil Zátopek. Since I took full notes of his evidence, I can quote. In reply to the question, what did he know about the preparation of the 'Ten Points' in 1969, Zátopek stated: 'When Pachman gave me the 'Ten Points' to read, I was horrified. I told him at once that he would be gaoled for this, and my sole reason for signing was not to let him get into trouble alone. Evidently he intended to circulate the document publicly. I cannot now recall whether he wanted to send it to the press. I said repeatedly to Luděk: "How can you carry on this disruptive activity? Why you even want to depose officers of state!" ' His lengthy, rambling statement continued in this vein, and when pressed by the judge to give a straight answer to my question, why had he signed a document he now described as disruptive, he finally solved the dilemma by putting the blame on Euženie! She had, it seemed, browbeaten him into signing!

When Dr. Lakatoš, also one of those who had worked on the first draft of the 'Ten Points', was called we had a demonstration of how a skilled lawyer can handle a situation. Having withdrawn his signature after my arrest, he was able to parry the question whether he had signed by stating truthfully, that he had not been a signatory to the document which had been presented to the authorities. Questioned about his participation in the drafting, he replied: 'Your honour, with regard to this question, I would avail myself of the indulgence offered by Article 100, which allows me to refuse to testify should I thereby place myself or those related to me in danger of prosecution.' The final question to this witness turned out badly for the prosecution. When asked about his relationship with the defendant, Pachman, and his opinion of the latter's activity at the time concerned, he no longer invoked Article 100. In a 10–15 minute speech, he said that he had been, and still was, a close friend of the defendant. Pachman was dedicated to the ideals of socialism, and always upheld these ideals with sincerity. Pachman's was a modern concept of socialism, corresponding to European traditions and conditions of life. And still more praise was heaped upon me.

The proceedings continued next day with further statements; then the prosecutor rose to deliver his summing up. He spoke precisely on the lines of the indictment as if nothing whatever had been said during the two days' hearing. Defence counsel, on the other hand, skilfully demolished the prosecution's arguments concerning both subversion and incitement. Finally, I spoke from a written statement, which I entered for the record. In opening, however, I replied to the prosecutor's allegation that I regarded the socialist system with hatred. This distressed me because 'I hold socialism to be a civilized order of society, and I shall not change my opinion even after my recent unhappy experiences . . . I acted solely in accordance with my conscience and my convictions. . . . Not being a politician, however, but a chess player, I was often guided in my pronouncements more by emotion than by rational judgement. . . .'

Having dealt with the points of the indictment, I added in conclusion that I intended to devote myself to chess, to getting well, and to my family. My last sentence was: 'The times are none too peaceful at present, history alone will pass final judgement on events.' The hearing was then adjourned until the afternoon when the verdict was to be pronounced.

In the interim, I was taken in handcuffs to the cell. As I was eating my lunch, the door flew open and a warder shot in. Instinctively, I assumed a defensive stance, but the man held out his hand, saying: 'I want to shake hands with you so you'll know there are decent people even here!' Then he hurried out, probably afraid that his colleagues might see him.

When the court reassembled all present rose to hear the judge announce: 'Hear the verdict in the name of the Republic!' The defendant was found guilty and sentenced to two years' imprisonment, to be served in the first grade. In the judge's statement of the grounds for the verdict, two points interested me— first, the case for my having read the 'Ten Points' at the camp fire was declared not proven; second, my radio interview was denoted as an act of incitement because it had been recorded in the presence of two Czechoslovak citizens, Jan Vlk and Jan Šling (despite the defence argument that since I had spoken in German, which neither of the other two understood, incitement was impossible).

Defence counsel asked whether a decision had been made about his proposal concerning my release. The judge replied that the court's decision would be announced, but first the defendant was required to reply to the   erdict. I consulted briefly with defence counsel—the incitement point was absurd—next time we might try inciting the people of Prague in Chinese. But should I appeal? One could hardly expect a shorter sentence, and to appeal might spoil my chances of release. I stood up to say: 'Mr. Chairman, I accept the verdict and I relinquish the right to appeal.'

Then the judge announced his decision—I was to be released. Had the prosecutor any comment, would he lodge an objection? No. EužEnie cried out, she rushed towards me and confusion reigned. A guard tried to halt her, she let fly at him, why couldn't she go to me now I was free? He insisted that I was not yet officially released, and he would hand me over after they had taken me to Pankrác for the necessary paper work to be done. The doors were opened, people were peering in from the corridor, and EužEnie went out to answer their questions. In the confusion the foreign journalists misunderstood what release from detention signified. They reported that my sentence had been commuted, but that was not the case—I could be called upon to serve the remaining six months at any time, the release was purely on grounds of health.

They drove me to Pankrác without handcuffs, and for the first time the warders talked to me as an equal. That was a marvellous feeling. I forgave them the handcuffs, they were simply obeying orders and, anyhow, there was that revealing incident during the adjournment.

The procedure lasted no more than twenty minutes, EužEnie was waiting, and we drove home to a warm welcome. As she was about to pour me a drink, I told her of my resolve to abstain from alcohol, that being part of my effort to surmount the physical according to the precepts of Thomas à Kempis. Then the phone started ringing and it was Dick Verkijk calling from Amsterdam. The news of my release had been broadcast an hour before, he wanted to give us his best wishes. In view of my promise in court, I let Euženie take that call. A friend of my wife called from Moravia having heard the news on the BBC.

Soon Euženie was giving me an account of what had happened since my arrest. First, of course, she recounted her battles with the Security police, including the house search, and also the story of our savings book. I had had it on me, but I asked the police to hand it to my wife. Yet, although it was in her name, they retained it. Consequently, Euženie stopped paying the bills, announcing to all concerned what she was not paying and directing that the bills be sent to Security for the attention of my interrogator. After that they returned the book in a hurry.

As we talked about this and that, friends phoned at intervals, most of them saying they would visit us next day.

23. Home

This time my first visitor was Ludvík. I told him frankly that he looked terrible with a beard, he argued that at least in that matter he had a right to freedom, so would I kindly not interfere. I retorted that I was all for freedom, but the beard was really impossible. I poured him a whisky, and an orange juice for myself. He watched me in amazement, then asked what was up. On hearing that I had gone off alcohol, he calmly poured the whisky back into the bottle—luckily, he takes it neat!—announcing with distaste: 'Well, in that case I'll have orange juice, too. I don't see why I should let you make yourself out to be a better man than me.'

He wouldn't listen to reason. He sat thinking for a while, then he stood up and sat down again. Finally, he said: 'You know, it's a queer business really. Everyone's been put inside, only I haven't. Soon people won't trust me and they'll be keeping their mouths shut when I'm around.'

I voiced my doubts about anyone keeping his mouth shut in Ludvík's presence; as for the rest, I could only hope his wish might be fulfilled because a spell in custody would work wonders for his growing paunch. We debated the problem of paunches for a while, then we just argued as usual about anything and everything.

Other friends came, they congratulated me on having slimmed again, and only the most outspoken hinted gently that I had aged a bit. That really hadn't struck me because I am not in the habit of looking in the mirror. When I did take a look I saw that they were right.

Otherwise, life was back to normal, with the usual worries. A lot of my time was occupied with visits to doctors, treatment for my damaged spine being the prime consideration. A week after my return home, I visited a country priest who was a friend of mine. Surprisingly, Ludvík accompanied me. We stayed over-night and rose at five, as was the custom there. Half an hour's meditation in the church preceded breakfast, then we had some free time to walk in the woods with the priest. Ludvík grumbled about the cold and the Spartan régime. In an informal manner the father heard my confession. I felt that on the last occasion, in January of the previous year, I had not done justice to thirty years of sinful life. And, of course, the main concern was to cure all the confusions of the Pankrác days. Then, when I had received absolution, the three of us walked and debated together.

During the next few days I had to start an entirely new occu-pation. After the nervous shock she had suffered through my arrest, my mother-in-law was not fit to do the cooking and, in the doctor's opinion, she would never be fit again. Since my wife was at work, I had to take on the job. The experience of my years as a boy scout came in handy, and still more a cookery book published in 1950. Since I had an idea, however, that butter, eggs and so on used to be pretty scarce in those days, I adjusted the quantities in the recipes accordingly—consequently, most of my dishes were swimming in fat.

Cooking is not at all a bad job—indeed, men are said by some to be handier at it than women. But that is far from true of shopping. I usually found that I was the only man among crowds of women, and I seemed to be alone, too, in my constant grumb-ling. It started with meat. At the outset of my career as a cook I was determined to work systematically. So I drew up a week's menu. While doing so I remembered having read, during my first spell in prison, an article in *Rudé právo* expatiating on the unhealthy effects of consuming pork. So I omitted pork from my menu. This was partly out of consideration for Ucho as well, since, in a handbook entitled 'Do You Keep a Cat?', Miroslav Soukup, otherwise known as a composer of chess problems, in-sists that pork is not good for cats.

For the first week, then, I chose veal with mushrooms, sirloin of beef, stewed beef, veal cutlets and other good things. The first day failed to work according to plan because the butcher was shut on Mondays. So I served fried cauliflower, although that, too, presented problems because there was a long queue outside the shop bearing the sign 'Vegetables and Fruit'. Presumably this would be the case only on the days when 'Meat: Fresh and Smoked' was closed, and that belief prevented me from grumbling overmuch while standing in this, my first proper queue.

On Tuesday morning I was at the butcher's before eight, but that did not save me from queueing. Progress was slow and I disapproved of the way the women shoppers held up business by chatting with the manager. Reaching the counter at last, I requested three-quarters of a kilogramme of veal (reckoning 200 grammes each for the adults and 150 for Ucho). The manager stood amazed—no, he had no veal. Making a rapid mental adjustment of the menu, I asked for sirloin. That, too, was not to be had. Pork, I was informed, was the only meat on sale. I protested that there ought to be a notice to that effect outside the shop—a remark which was not deemed worthy of notice, so I withdrew in disgust, asking the last lady in the queue to direct me to a butcher's where I could buy veal and beef.

First, the lady looked me over as if I were some exotic being, then she informed me that I wouldn't find any beef at the moment and there had been no veal for about two years.

The news filled me with indignation. Returning to the other side of the counter, I demanded that the manager explain why *Rudé právo* recommended cutting down on pork consumption when there was no other meat to be had. At first he was somewhat taken aback by the mention of the paper, but soon he waxed unusually communicative so that, after a brief discussion, the matter was elucidated. It seemed that in 1970 when I had read the health notes, there had been plenty of beef on the market and no pork. Now the reverse was the case. Naturally, nobody wrote now about pork being harmful, on the contrary, the Sunday editions of the paper offered an abundance of recipes for tasty dishes based on pork.

The manager rejected my view that he ought to protest. He argued that it was his job to sell the goods he received, that he did so successfully and it would certainly not pay him to protest. I would have liked to give him a piece of my mind, but remembering my charge under Article 100, I decided to refrain, for the present, from incitement. But I did marvel at all those women standing patiently in the queues, all buying pork without a murmur, although without a doubt not one of them can have heard about the provisions of Article 100. I suppose they are used to these things.

Worse was in store for me, however. The queue at 'Vegetables and Fruit' was not merely on Mondays, it was every day. At the self-service shop it was shorter but one had to wait twice: once to acquire an empty basket, and again at the check-out. I grumbled loudly, thereby moving two of the women present to utter remarks which the prosecutor would undoubtedly have classified as incitement motivated by hatred of the socialist state and the socialist order of our Republic (Article 100, para. 1). I am not sure if he would have had a case against myself for abetting the commission of an offence—but, on second thoughts, he would because he's no need to find grounds for a case when he's a mind to make one.

Recalling my rights as a citizen of a socialist country, I started demanding the complaints books which are available in all institutions. A lively correspondence ensued, in the course of which various area managements informed me about the causes of their temporary shortages.

By this time I was falling behind with my reading programme, and altogether I was finding difficulty in combining life at home with being in the wilderness. Among our frequent visitors were a number of women, because most of the men in our immediate circle were in prison. There had been a big round-up in January, some people being charged with producing election leaflets and four seemed likely to be charged with the 'Ten Points' as well, but as a secondary matter, whereas in my case they constituted the main item.

The prisoners' wives used to gather, sometimes in one or the other of their homes, sometimes in ours. Somehow Eužénie had retained the right to belong to the group, although I had

187

christened it the League of Deserted Wives. Now and then I joined them to enable my wife to take a drink without fear of the traffic police. The main item on the agenda at these meetings was reading letters from prison and weighing up their contents. To add to all the other worries, almost all the men were in very poor health. So I was subjected to searching interrogations—what were the cells like, what did the windows look out on to, what did one wear, what was there for breakfast, dinner, supper, what was the temperature in the cells? Under interrogation of that nature one realizes how many things one has failed to notice. I tried to cheer things up by cooking festive meals when the meetings were at our place, though it was none too easy to shop for the dishes I planned.

At the children's home, things were bad for us. Milan and Jana were forbidden to visit us. The head of the home told us that it was not her idea, the order had come from the local council, the reason given being that our influence would not be in harmony with State policy. That meant that our visits to the home were also forbidden, although we went there now and then when the headmistress was out. Once, however, Euženie and Milan had the misfortune to meet her on their way back from buying a birthday cake which they were taking to the home so that Jana could share the treat. I put the matter in the hands of a lawyer with a suggestion that we foster the children, but there seemed little hope. The provisions about fostering include something about education in the socialist spirit, and I fear I really do not understand the kind of socialism to which they refer.

Early in June a gentleman phoned to say he wanted to talk to me about the possibility of a pardon to cover the remainder of my sentence. I intimated that I had no objection, and he added that his superior officer would accompany him.

When the two comrades arrived, I offered them drinks. They chose vodka although I had put out a bottle of Queen Mary whisky to shake their ideological loyalty. First, they inquired about my health, eliciting the information that I was receiving injections every second day, and I would have to wear a corset to support my spine, which was an unpleasant prospect in the hot weather we were having. They nodded gravely, expressing the hope that the condition would improve. The higher-ranking comrade then remarked that I ought to turn once more to Marxism, because 'one has to believe in something'. While agreeing entirely with the latter proposition, I added that Marxism did not seem to me to fulfil the need. That saddened him. Since he was obviously seeking a new line of conversation, I thought it better to ask straight out why they had come.

'Well, you see the Ministry of Justice is considering the question of pardoning you the rest of your sentence. In that connection we have to put in a report about your present activity, that will be decisive in deciding the case. And what we put in the report will depend on how frank you are with us.'

The penny did not drop at once—I said merely that I had nothing to conceal, I was writing a book on chess and I had taken over the editorship of the Hamburg journal *Schach-Archiv*, the fees for which were transferred quite legally through the bank— since I had no employment in Czechoslovakia, they provided my livelihood.

The officer smiled, saying they knew all about that. Of course, he omitted to mention that they had the information from my telephone calls and my letters, but obviously he knew that I knew.

I remarked that there was nothing more to say because I was not engaged in any other activity.

'We're not interested in *your* activity,' he said.

Now it was clear what they wanted, but I thought I would pick their brains a bit before throwing them out. So I said, as if in surprise, that what other people did could surely have no bearing on whether or not I was to be put in prison.

'It is precisely a question of how frank you are that can influence the matter of your pardon.' He sat back affably, crossing his legs as he explained: 'We don't want much, and it'll hurt no one. For a start, just one thing. In October last year in the Kyncls' apartment, in the presence of five people including your wife, you offered to arrange for an interview with Josef Smrkovský to be duplicated. You said you knew someone whose brother had access to a duplicator at his place of work. We are interested in one thing—your friend's name.'

So now we knew—the Kyncls' place had been bugged. Luckily, when I talk away from home, I don't mention names. Now I enjoyed crossing my legs as I asked if he thought he would get that information. He said he thought he should because it would help me and, he added, 'You must think of your wife, she's in it, too, and if you don't tell us, we'll have to interrogate her.'

That shot misfired, because Euženie would have enjoyed herself—in talking to Security men she adopts the peremptory tone of a superior dealing with subordinates.

'I can assure you', I said, 'that my friend, or rather his brother, was a bit nervous, so he did nothing and there is no need for you to take any further interest in the matter.'

That, he replied affably, was not the case. Their job was to have everything 'mapped out', whatever happened. That, I replied, was an idea which did not appeal to me, and I would have nothing to do with it. Settling back in the armchair, he informed me that he would not leave until I had told him this one trifling thing. At that, I rose, saying that I must cook the dinner, I had no intention of going hungry on their account. Finally, they gave up, but on the way out the head man seized me by the lapel of my jacket as he fired his parting shot—was I really determined not to tell them anything?'

For some days nothing happened. I worked on my book, friends came and went, and we made a trip to Smrkovský's country cottage to inquire after his health. On 13 July we celebrated my mother-in-law's birthday, her sixty-ninth. I recalled the promise that we would celebrate every round number somewhere in the south, but the seventieth would not, alas, be in Spain as planned because things wouldn't have changed by then.

To the birthday dinner in Prague's Chinese restaurant we invited three members of the Deserted Wives League. First we went to the cinema. Unfortunately, the show I had chosen was not very cheerful—it was an English film about the French Revolution, which was currently something of a sensation in

Prague because of the abuse of revolution put into the mouth of the Marquis de Sade, with Marat, on the other hand, stoutly defending its principle. I found myself thinking, rather sadly, that in the old days I would have been wholly on Marat's side, whereas now I was more in sympathy with the cynical wisdom of de Sade. Certainly it was not the best entertainment for my mother-in-law and the prisoners' wives—I should have chosen a comedy.

The depression was dispelled, however, over dinner. The waiters, knowing that we were celebrating something, served us with the very best they had to offer.

Next day, a car drove up to our house. The plain-clothes men who rang our bell told me they had come to take me to head-quarters, just for a talk.

Three officers were waiting to receive me. They told me that I had broken the undertaking made in court since I was engaging once more in subversive activity and gathering anti-State elements around myself. To my expression of surprise and demand for a more definite statement, they responded at first in the manner of all less intelligent interrogators by saying that I must know better than they what was involved. But my suggestion that we might as well end the interview moved them to come out with an accusation: 'Well, yesterday evening, for instance, you were at the Chinese restaurant with three wives of prisoners. That is nothing less than a public provocation.' I remarked that one could also see it as a celebration of my mother-in-law's birthday, but that they refused to accept. I had been told to make no public appearance. The debate grew heated as I insisted that a dinner is not a public appearance, at the most it is public consumption. Moreover, I had never promised to desert my friends and the three women certainly needed to be cheered up a bit.

Another accusation followed: 'We know that you are giving financial support to families of people in prison. That can be classified as condoning criminal activity as defined by the Penal Code.' I wondered how women with young children could manage to engage in anti-State activity, and how was Mrs.

Tesář supposed to support her family of three without some help from friends, since the Government showed no concern.

'That's not your worry,' I was told.

I said that I would be only too glad to leave the worry to them —perhaps they would like to start straightaway. Incensed by my untimely remark, they now intimated that they had much more information—for instance, I had visited Smrkovský. This, they told me in conclusion, was the last warning, next time they would 'proceed to action'. In all, the interview lasted some two and a half hours, the main theme being interspersed with minor arguments on subjects such as history, philosophy and politics.

That was on Friday; the action commenced on the Monday. Setting out shortly before eight to do the shopping, I found a Volga standing just up the street and another car near by. Two men from the Volga followed me at a distance of about ten feet. When we arrived at our local self-service store, they stood by the door watching as I made my way along the shelves. The temptation to watch them was too strong, and it could have been my downfall, for I discovered that I had blindly put half my purchases into my shopping bag in place of the self-service basket. Luckily I managed to correct the error before reaching the cashier, but I felt quite faint at the thought of what would have happened if they had been able to pounce on me for stealing five tins of soup, two of Chinese pork and half a pound of cheese.

On the way home I made a bad mistake by cutting across our garden from the street behind our house and entering by the back door, which had not previously been guarded. Within twenty minutes a car was parked there, too.

As always, neighbours came to report on the situation among the encircling forces. A student discovered an excellent way of escaping the watchful eyes. Entering a house a few doors from us with a casual air, he then traversed the gardens to the shelter of our veranda, which was screened by bushes. He offered his services—did we need anything taken anywhere or what could he do?

The weather being terribly hot, I had planned to go swimming, but reports about how the watchdogs were sweating—some with their shirts off and fanning themselves with *Rudé právo*—caused me to change my mind. If I went, they would go too, probably charging entrance tickets and refreshments to expenses. So let them sweat. I took a shower now and then while working on my book about the Fischer-Spassky match.

In Reykjavik things were even livelier than around our house. The match had been due to start on 2 July, but Fischer had not arrived. Three times he had been sighted at New York airports, only to leave again. He informed the organizers that a trifling $150,000 was not nearly enough for himself and Spassky. That caused commotion all round the world until an English millionaire, Mr. Slater, decided to save the match by donating another £50,000.

The affair shocked me—formerly world champions had been happy to pocket $5,000. Not that I grudged Bobby his earnings, but it struck me as out of place for a man to agree, through his representatives, to conditions and then to try to extract more at the last minute. In a pretty sharp commentary for *Deutsche Schachblätter*, I praised Mr. Slater for his generosity while suggesting that, in a world where two-thirds of the population go hungry, it could have been put to much better use.

When Ludvík came to see us on the Wednesday, he said my attitude was crazy, the £50,000 had saved an interesting match and, anyhow, let people squander money if they liked. We also discussed why the gang was constantly haunting our doorway. Six or seven were on duty from seven in the morning till seven in the evening, when the night-shift took over. And as I never went out, they could not even enjoy the diversion of shadowing me. Ludvík was of the opinion that it was pointless to seek a reason, as they simply did things for something to do, or to make people aware of them, or to assure themselves that they were necessary to socialism. I felt that there might be some connection with the fact that some of the detainees were now on trial, among them Husák's one-time friend, Dr. Hübl, former student leader Jiří Müller, my friend the historian, Dr. Tesář, and the former M.P., Rudolf Battěk. Since the last two were charged, among other things, with the matter of the 'Ten Points', some relevance to myself might be seen.

Next day I set to work on a plan which had occurred to me in the intervals between commenting on Fischer's games. First, I wrote a seven-page letter to the Minister of the Interior, giving a detailed account of my experiences over the past three years with the departments under his jurisdiction. I requested that I be provided with the necessary documents to allow myself and my family to emigrate. In conclusion, I wrote: 'In the light of my experiences of recent years, I fear that this case will be handled in the manner which is, alas, customary with your departments. I would therefore point out that all documents, including a translation of this letter, are prepared for submission to the Committee for Human Rights at the United Nations.' The last assertion was premature because I started preparing the documents two or three days after sending the letter, but I was confident that the bureaucracy would not operate with undue speed.

My next letter was to the Minister of Justice with reference to notification I had received from the court that I was to be charged for the costs of eighteen months' detention to the tune of close on 20,000 Czechoslovak crowns. I now intimated that I would present a counter-claim to the Ministry. Comparison of X-ray photographs taken before 1969, in December 1969, and later, showed that inadequate treatment given in the prison hospital to the spinal fracture I suffered in December '69 had left me with a permanent deformation of three vertebrae, causing me recurrent pain and reducing my working capacity. I suggested that the Minister might, perhaps, prefer to forget the bill for detention charges.

Money was not the primary consideration although the sum involved was far from negligible. The point of the haggling emerged in my third letter addressed to the head of Pankrác Prison hospital, whom I informed that I had on loan from them X-ray records which showed . . . etc. 'And,' I wrote, 'in view of the fact that our doctors are presently somewhat inhibited in their freedom of judgement by fears for their livelihood, I have sent the photographs for medical opinion abroad.'

My wife delivered the letter to the Minister of the Interior by hand—the following day the watchdogs had vanished from our street. And soon Security men were inquiring among the doctors as to the whereabouts of my X-ray records. One doctor, replying to a brusque question about the Pachman photos, asked calmly:
'Which Pachman?'

'What, don't you know Pachman?' the officer exclaimed.

'I ask you, how can I know all my patients? Wait a moment ... Pachman, yes, I know two of them. Which do you mean?'

The head of the Pankrác hospital hastened to write demanding the return of the photos by 15 September, failing which he would lay a charge of theft of official records. My lawyer laughed heartily—that would be a novelty, a patient stealing his own records! But I was not amused, obviously things were getting tough. I had copies made, and arranged for my lawyer to deliver them, but after 15 September to avoid giving the impression that we had been intimidated by the threat.

While all this was happening I was also working on the Reykjavik book. Fischer played the first game as if he wanted to add interest to the match—he let his bishop get caught in the endgame, and he lost. For the second game, he failed to put in an appearance because he was quarrelling with the organizers about the television cameras, which was a headache for them since they counted on the payments from TV companies to help cover their costs. The score stood at 2–0 to Spassky, which caused the *Rudé právo* commentators to rejoice at the prospect of a triumph for the USSR. Personally, I would have liked to see Spassky win (he is a fine chap, as I've already said), but Soviet triumphs were not much to my taste. This presented me with some problems in writing my commentaries for *Deutsche Schachblätter*. In Spassky's place I would have castled busily, pushed everything to a draw and hoped that would put Fischer off his game. But Spassky was anxious to decide the match right in the third game, and wipe the floor with Fischer. Bobby, however, is a troublesome, but also a brilliant player. He won a beautiful game, then another, and the two were neck and neck.

For a full four weeks not a word came from the Ministers.

When I phoned I was informed that the Minister of the Interior was on holiday, and he would certainly reply on his return. In the meantime I had had time to think things over and consult my friends. Obviously, it would be risky to go ahead with a venture I had embarked on without much thought, having conceived the idea in the intervals between writing. If I now kept quiet, maybe everything would blow over. But what sort of a life would it be? Hemmed in all the time, shadowed, with no chance of doing anything worth while. Political activity would be madness, and irresponsible because I would put others in danger. After my second term in prison,friends had advised me to concentrate on getting well, but how can one get well when there is always something to be upset about?

Finally, I decided to go ahead. So now I wrote to the Presidium of the Communist Party, enclosing a brief summary of my letter to the Minister. First, I pointed out that while I could understand journalism being closed to me, that was not the case with chess, to which I had devoted the greater part of my life. Although the authorities had the right not to select me for the national team, I was at a loss to know why I could not play in events where I would represent myself alone, or why I was barred from even belonging to a club. And I continued: 'In the entire history of the game, no player has previously been expelled from his Federation on political grounds. For instance, in our country chessmaster F. J. Prokop was not expelled, although he was editor of a pro-Nazi paper during the war and received a five-year sentence for collaboration. Nor was grandmaster Sämisch expelled from the Great German Chess Federation although, as an anti-fascist, he was sent to a concentration camp.'

My wife, too, had been dismissed from her post for political reasons, and now she was threatened with dismissal from the entirely unpolitical job she had managed to find, solely on account of my name. Moreover, the reasons given for my two terms of detention—first, my part in preparing the 'Ten Points', and second, the Dutch radio interview—referred solely to the fact that I had openly stated my opinions, and the main charge, on which I was ultimately convicted, related to my political activity in 1969 (despite repeated promises by our leading statesmen that no one would be penalized for his activity in 1968–9).

On returning from prison, on both occasions, I continued, I had been sincerely resolved to avoid any kind of political involvement, to devote myself to regaining my health and to chess. In the previous year, however, a crude campaign against me by the media had made it impossible to adhere to my resolve, while in the present year the security police had been subjecting me to what could only be termed gross intimidation. My health had been seriously affected by my terms in prison, yet I was evidently not to be allowed the rest and freedom from worry which my condition required. Obviously, my very existence was an embarrassment to the authorities and involved them in considerable expense. By granting my application to emigrate, such expenditure would be saved, as well as my disability pension and my mother-in-law's pension. In conclusion, I demanded either to be allowed to lead a normal life in Czechoslovakia—which, in the case of a grandmaster of chess, should certainly be considered to include his right to play chess—or that I be given permission to emigrate. Finally, I alluded to the threat that if I failed to get a satisfactory response the matter would be laid before various international institutions.

The following days were crowded with chess affairs. Herr Rattmann arrived from Hamburg with numerous requests concerning the *Schach-Archiv*, the Fischer-Spassky book was to be published a month after the match ended and to be exhibited at the Frankfurt Book Fair, while contributions to various foreign journals were also required. I was fully occupied. Fees started coming in and that led me to expect another onslaught from the media, including, by all accounts, a television film designed to expose me as a thorough rascal. The idea was to contrast my statements in the '50s with those of more recent times. Not a very brilliant device, I felt, since I had often declared that I was stupid in those days—that was nothing new. It seemed that this film was to have been shown at the time of my trial, but someone at the top and stopped it at the last moment.

In the rush of work I had no time for a holiday. Moreover,

Euženie had problems owing to the threat of dismissal from the building co-operative where she was employed. Their central office insisted that Mrs. Pachman could not be allowed to work as a secretary, knowing everything that went on in the place, and really she should not be employed at all, it could only cause trouble. But her immediate boss unexpectedly stood firm. He was a decent fellow who, being a Party member, had got the job when the order went out that such posts could not be held by non-members. His predecessor, an expert but not a Party man, had to content himself with a subordinate post. Now the new chief maintained that Mrs. Pachman was a good worker, and he had no reason to sack her. To the threat that his attitude might cost him his job, he replied that he could go back to his trade on a building site, he would not suffer financially and he would have less worry. So, thanks to his stand, the matter was again postponed. Many people contend that there is no alternative to obeying orders from the top, even if it means sacking a fellow worker. To say one 'has to' is a poor excuse, however. It is because everyone thinks they 'have to' that we suffer a régime which behaves in the manner of a feudal overlord. Were people to stop thinking this way, the régime would be impossible.

Five days after sending the letter to the Party I had a phone call from a Colonel at the Ministry of the Interior. Being empowered by the Minister to deal with the matters I had raised, he wished to visit me. He came accompanied by a second officer. Remembering the previous occasion, I offered vodka, remarking that whisky was not popular, so I understood, in their department. The Colonel was upset, he became very official and refused even coffee. Then he got down to business:

'Comrade Minister has empowered me to say that he objects to the tone of your letter and considers it to be out of place and offensive.'

A fine beginning! Naturally, I started arguing about what is offensive, citing examples of the methods used by the authorities. He interrupted me:

'We haven't come to hold a political debate. I am to inform you that, thanks to the magnanimity of the political bodies

concerned, you will, nevertheless, be enabled to leave Czechoslovakia with your family.'

I asked if this was official—yes, it was. No, they would not
give me the decision in writing, Comrade so-and-so—he pointed
to his companion—would explain the procedure for applying to
the Passport Office, and my application would be granted.
Whereupon the comrade spoke at length about all the certificates
and documents I would require—for instance, I would have to
obtain a statement from the district military headquarters that
they had no objection to my departure. The main requirement,
however, was that I sign a declaration renouncing all property I
might possess in Czechoslovakia at the time of leaving. Finally,
I would have to pay charges according to the regulations, ranging
from 400 to 10,000 crowns.

My first thought after their departure was that it might be a
hoax, so I immediately dispatched a letter to the Minister confirming the verbal agreement reached with his representative. I
had barely finished writing when the phone rang. Koblenc
calling. Herr Leicher of *Rhein-Zeitung* asked if I would be willing
to give an interview on the Fischer-Spassky match. Rapidly
debating in my mind whether my undertaking not to give interviews to foreign papers could be expected to apply to non-
political matters, I decided that in any case the Security people
had broken their side of the bargain by treating me as a dangerous
criminal once more. Therefore, I repeated my view that Bobby
would hold the world champion title for, say, ten years. I spoke
warmly about Boris's personal qualities, commented on the start
of the match and mentioned my own encounters with Fischer.
When I had finished, Herr Leicher said he had one more request
—readers would welcome signed copies of my books on chess,
they could send a consignment to Prague for me to sign and
return.

'You can do that,' I told him, 'but if there's no hurry, it would
be better to wait. In about two months' time I should be able to
sign them at your offices.'

That was evidently a bombshell. Herr Leicher showered me
with questions—was I sure it was true? Where did I plan to live?

And so on. I said I would probably go to Holland, but it was too early to say definitely, it depended on many things, primarily on who would want me.

An hour later the Prague correspondent of the German DPA rang: 'Mr. Pachman, we have just received a message from head office saying that, according to information obtained by a German paper, you have been given permission to leave Czechoslovakia. Is that correct?'

I confirmed the report. Within an hour Reuter was on the line, and in the evening, just four hours after the interview with *Rhein-Zeitung*, came Agence France Presse—they had received a telex from head office. . . .

So now it was out. Should the Minister, or a super-Minister at Party headquarters, or an even superior personage at the Soviet Embassy have second thoughts, there would at least be some sort of outcry abroad, and when one is inside, an outcry is the only hope. For I saw just two ways for them to handle my case— either they could let me go, or they would shut me up again. They would be arguing about it now.

I embarked on a round of visits to offices, which proved a most interesting experience. The officials were usually very pleasant and helpful. Some even glanced over their shoulders, leant towards me, and delivered remarks which would be indictable under Article 100 except for the circumstance that the Article required two witnesses and I was alone.

Before signing away my property to the State, I did what I could to get rid of it. We had our house valued, but our hopes of selling it were dashed by the discovery of a Government order to the effect that 'the sale of property concluded with intent to avoid legal obligation can be declared invalid.' And the provisions for executing the order stated that 'this measure applies particularly in cases where the sale is concluded less than one year before leaving the Republic'. Originally, the provision referred to illegal escape, but as that was not explicitly stated, there was no getting round it. So the State would get the house for nothing; but I would take some of the gilt off the gingerbread—I had a plan for doing that. Having studied the law a bit, I drew up a document whereby Mr. and Mrs. Pachman sued the Czecho-slovak State on the grounds that, in contravention of two articles of the Constitution and several provisions of the Civil Code, advantage had been taken of their difficult situation to compel them to sign a declaration renouncing their property. The said declaration, therefore, had no legal validity and was, moreover, an infringement of the Charter of Human Rights, to which Czechoslovakia was a signatory. At the same time we entered into a contract with a working class family with three young children and no home of their own. We placed the house at their disposal free of charge for the duration of our stay abroad, undertaking to rehouse them suitably on our return. The thought struck me, incidentally, that when that day came, there would be plenty of people with nice apartments who would be anxious to leave the country.

The final formality was to obtain the certificate from the military authorities. Not being on the reserve, I assumed it to be a matter I could leave till last since the defence capacity of the Warsaw Pact would not be lessened one iota on my departure. But the Army is the Army—the first office I entered sent me to another where they informed me that they dealt only with officers and NCOs, so they passed me on to the place where they handled the rank and file. There, having heard my request, they announced that since I was not in the Army I was no concern of theirs. Moreover, they insisted, very logically, no military depart-ment could provide a certificate for a civilian like myself. They were unmoved by my contention that, in view of the fact that the Ministry of the Interior required it, the thing must be possible.

The commanding officer of the district headquarters, to whom I then applied, pondered deeply, then he asked to see the docu-ment releasing me from military service. At that I had to confess that, although I had received a paper of that nature some twenty-five years previously, I had lost it—in any case, my identity card recorded that I was not on the reserve. The officer then in-structed me to report the said loss in the third office down the passage.

Entering this office to make my report, I was received by two officers and a young lady. The more important officer wanted me to apply to the police to find my document. I replied that, without wishing to belittle the skill of our police force, I doubted if they could find an article which had been lost some twenty-five years previously. The man was the image of Lieutenant Dub in *The Good Soldier Schweik*—his arguments were comic, and his colleagues laughed surreptitiously into their files.

When I returned to the commander to inform him of my inability to carry out his order, he led me back to Lieutenant Dub, to whom he issued an instruction that my report be received. Having recorded my name, date of birth and so on, this officer concluded by saying 'All right'. I retorted that it was not all right, because I needed the certificate—and that cost me a third visit to the commander, who again accompanied me and issued the appropriate order. Dub replied, 'Yes sir,' then, frowning greatly, he wrote that I was 'allegedly not on the reserve' and had reported the loss of a military document. My polite request that he add a sentence about there being no objection to my leaving the country sparked off a heated debate, ending with him shouting: 'You have objections to our socialist régime, what?' When I remarked that it was more a matter of the régime having objections to me, he rushed to fetch the commander who, looking rather bored, asked: 'What have you been saying about our Government?' I explained that the Government had no great liking for me, so I wanted to oblige by leaving the country. 'Well, write that we have no objection,' said the commander.

On leaving, I bowed saying, 'Thank you very much and goodbye till next time.' That elicited an angry 'Hope there won't be one,' from Lieutenant Dub, but the young lady smiled at me.

Eužénie and I paid one more visit to the local council office, where on the previous day the department head had recorded his disagreement with our departure. We went to ask his reason. He explained that he knew me, having once held a post in physical training, and he had once presented me with an award. In his view I was of an age to be of value to the country, therefore it was not right that I should leave. His concern was, indeed, touching but I had to point out that his boss, the Minister of the Interior, took a different view.

Finally, we repaired to the appropriate department to hand in all the forms, decorated with a variety of rubber stamps. An important lady refused at first to accept them, objecting that emigration was open exclusively to women marrying foreigners, or to pensioners who would be cared for by someone abroad. My suggestion that she ring the Minister silenced her on that point, but she frowned, then asked: 'Of course, you are renouncing your Czechoslovak nationality?' Replying that, of course, I would retain my nationality, I pointed to the conclusion of my application, where I had written that I intended to return as soon as conditions were back to normal. Without further comment, the lady informed me that I would be notified by post.

24. The Frontier

Now we had new worries. We had to sell most of our furniture and many books, arrange transport for our things, make a list for the customs people and, above all, watch our expenditure to avoid leaving debts behind us. The list for customs was a joke: we had to record every trifle to be dispatched by the transport firm, giving the make of each article, year of manufacture, and value. We had the interesting item: '*Article:* cat; *Make:* domestic cat named Ucho; *Value:* about 50 crowns.' The duty on her was assessed at a mere 1.50 crowns because she was judged to be of no known breed.

Again, journalists kept ringing from abroad, inquiring particularly where we intended to settle. For some time we were uncertain about this. On receiving the Minister's communication that he would be glad to see me go, I had written to the Dutch chess organization with two requests—to pass on my application for residence in Holland, and to help me re-enter the world of chess (for instance, by arranging a simultaneous display, or inviting me to play in a tournament). The answer came after six weeks. Six lines of laughable German informed me that they could do nothing for me. I recalled that Dr. Euwe owed me replies to four letters, and I knew what the trouble was. Although I had thousands of friends in Holland, I would not be welcomed by the chess potentates for the simple reason that, if I settled there, the Soviet players might cease to attend tournaments in Holland.

To digress for a moment, I may add that when I arrived in Holland, I gave a brief answer to the question why I was not planning to settle there. The letter from the Royal Dutch Chess Federation was shown on television, and the fat was in the fire. Indignant articles in the press were followed by voices from the other side. My friend Herr Donner wrote that peace is more important than freedom and, instead of bothering about Czechoslovakia, the Dutch should concern themselves with the West and problems such as Vietnam. The Soviet Union, he added, is the greatest power for peace. We had a debate on television about this. Another Dutch chess player discovered that I had first sympathized with the Nazis, then become a Stalinist, and now I was anti-communist. I filed a suit against him, but he retracted the day before the hearing, also apologizing to the newspaper concerned and paying the sum of 1,000 gulden to my lawyer and the court.

Almost simultaneously with the letter from Holland, I received, via Hamburg, an invitation from Solingen. Herr Evertz, chairman of the chess club there and my friend since 1968 had, on his own initiative, obtained permission for us to reside in West Germany, and also found an apartment and arranged other matters. So that was settled—we would live in Solingen.

We had many discussions with our friends about future plans. Some even considered trying to take advantage of the precedent set by my departure—we might establish a foreign branch of UCHO (our Centre of Czechoslovak Resistance), and perhaps build an UCHO co-operative house. But they all came up against obstacles in their families. As for Ludvík, he firmly rejected the idea. Once, as we were chatting, he suddenly remarked: 'That's odd, I've only just realized you won't be here.' As he spoke, I, too, felt my first pang of regret, but I changed the subject by weaving plans—in a fit of megalomania, as Ludvík said. My visions involved many countries, including those of the great Mao, Nixon and Brandt, and a time scale for a new phase of revival at home. Ludvík commented drily that I would do best to occupy myself with chess—in the West it was presumably necessary to earn one's living.

On 17 October, precisely at noon, we received a communication from the Passport Office acceding to our request to go abroad. For myself, the payment amounted to 10,000 crowns, for Eužénie the same sum, and 6,000 for my mother-in-law;

passports would be issued a week after receipt of the money. We paid it over the same day. Then we threw ourselves into the job of clearing up the apartment. The transport firm was to collect on 7 November, and we planned to travel that day—it would be a good celebration of the anniversary of the Russian Revolution— but the firm spoilt things by announcing that packing would take two days, which meant postponing our departure to the 8th. I booked rooms for that night in Bamberg. It struck me that another anniversary fell on that day, and very apt it was—the day in 1620 when the armies of Bohemia were defeated by the Hapsburgs at the Battle of the White Mountain.

On 24 October, when the week had elapsed, I visited the Passport Office. They sent me from the outer office to a more important one where a surprise awaited me. The matter had not yet been settled, I was told, and the official had no idea when it would be. But here, I objected, I have a communication stating that the matter has been decided, and we have paid the sum of 26,000 crowns as required. That he brushed aside, telling me brusquely not to bother him, they would write in due course, and I was not to inquire by telephone—they had other work to do.

At the Ministry of the Interior I asked to speak to the Minister's secretary who, having examined my documents quite pleasantly, promised to let me know within two or three days how things stood. When, on the third day, he telephoned, however, he informed me that there seemed to be a hitch, but he had been unable to discover what it was.

There was something odd in that. Who, I wondered, handled these matters if even the Minister's secretary was kept in the dark? In a fit of anger I sat down to write once more to the Party. In precise terms I informed them what I would do if they failed to put things right. The Minister of the Interior, I wrote, had obtained the sum of 26,000 crowns on false pretences, and, I added in conclusion: 'I am fully aware that by lodging this complaint I am exposing myself to the crude form of revenge which has become an integral part of your political system. Nevertheless, I refuse to be intimidated by the arrogant treatment meted out by the departments upon which your power rests.'

Now I was sure I had sealed my fate—they would have no alternative but to put me back in prison. Obviously, the odd behaviour at the Passport Office had been politically inspired: the leadership was divided on what to do with me, and probably the faction opposed to letting me go was persuading the others to change their minds. I hastened to inform the AFP and DPA press agencies that I had been tricked again by the authorities, who had pocketed the money and were withholding our passports. Then I made a translation of my letter to the Party, intending to send it abroad, but not by post.

For ten days we lived in uncertainty. Then came a summons to collect our passports, and we had to rush to get things done. Luckily the transport firm obliged by promising to pack on 15 and 16 November, enabling us to leave on the Thursday evening. We would spend the night at Selb, a town on the German frontier where I had deposited some savings from my chess earnings as a nest-egg on which I could draw when I travelled abroad—originally, it had been intended for our Spanish holiday. Now it would come in handy because the emigration allowance from our State Bank amounted to 25 DM per head, at the rate of 10 Czechoslovak crowns for 1 DM, whereas the West German tourist can exchange at the rate of 4:1.

An interesting point about the customs procedure, according to information I received, was that if one customs officer should accompany the men who packed our things, he would be a genuine customs man; should two come, one would be a Security officer—in our case, three men turned up. They evinced no interest in the nature of the goods—I could easily have exported pure gold in place of kitchen utensils—but they inspected every scrap of paper. Whether I could take with me the official court records and the prosecution statements had to be decided next day after they had consulted their boss. Certificates referring to educational qualifications, including Euženie's certificate as a figure-skating judge, were banned—personal documents could be sent abroad only through diplomatic channels.

Finally, we held a farewell dinner, to which we invited seven members of the Deserted Wives League, and one released husband—let the Security people gnash their teeth! Having dined in a wine restaurant in Prague's Little Quarter, we repaired to our house to drink toasts among the packing cases. We promised never to forget these friends of ours, nor their imprisoned menfolk. The women shed tears, as is their right. Ucho paid a last visit to the black cat on the hillside.

The following day, by four in the afternoon, packing was finished, the customs officials, or whatever they were, departed and we entertained the packers with wine and the last drops of slivovitz. We reckoned that we had just enough Czechoslovak money left to cover tips, supper before crossing the frontier, and tanking up the cars.

But—at four-thirty, the telephone rang. The Passport Office: 'Mr. Pachman, you have presumably overlooked the fact that you are not permitted to travel before 20 November. We are calling your attention to this to save you from making an unnecessary journey to the frontier.' True enough, on inspecting the exit permits, we found that although the date of issue was 20 October, in the space 'valid until' was inscribed 'from 20.11.1972 to 20.5.1973'. They must have invented the item 'from' for our benefit. I recalled that there would be elections in Germany on 19 November, and by all reports 300 prisoners had been allowed to return from East Germany prior to that date. Perhaps one ex-prisoner from Czechoslovakia was too much.

What now? The apartment was bare, we had no Czechoslovak money except what we had put aside to pay our gas, electricity and telephone bills. These Ludvík undertook to pay so that we could use our cash, and we slept with friends. Next morning we set out for the frontier because a night's lodging in Prague would have been beyond our means. We filled in the time in a small town on our route, then at 7.05 on the Monday morning we presented ourselves at the frontier post. Since our luggage had already been examined by the customs people and duly sealed, the formalities could have been over in five minutes. That, however, was not to be. We were shown into the customs office and left to wait for two hours. Then I was summoned by the head of passport control. We could not cross the frontier, he said, because on the other side in Germany provocative actions against me were to be expected. I asked what kind of action was meant and who was supposed to be responsible. He denied any knowledge of the circumstances, his orders were simply that we were to return immediately to Prague and report to the authorities there. My mother-in-law burst into tears when she heard the news—they would never let us go, I would be put into prison and what would become of us all. She was so distressed that we decided to leave her with acquaintances who lived near by while we took the road back to Prague. There we put Ucho into the empty apartment with a supply of food before booking a room for the night at the Praga Hotel. The reception clerk gave us a warm welcome for he was the writer, Alexander Klimentev, now banned from pursuing his profession.

At 4.00 p.m. precisely I presented myself with my lawyer at police headquarters. He could hardly believe what had happened, but during a wait of three-quarters of an hour he kept assuring me that all would be well. When the man from the Ministry arrived, we were summoned to appear. Presiding at the interview was the police commandant, who repeated what we had been told at the frontier post: namely, that it was their duty to protect us against trouble in Germany in view of the fact that we were still Czechoslovak nationals. We could leave at any time after midnight on 28 November.

In lodging my protest, I announced that I intended to report the whole affair to foreign news agencies—a statement which was not entirely true, because I had taken the step an hour previously. I also said that I would sue for damages occasioned by this mess up. Over the latter point they expressed understanding—they would pay for our accommodation at Hotel Flora, plus an appropriate sum to cover food and expenses. In reply I remarked that although according to the ancient Romans *pecunia non olet*, I I could not be sure about their money. I would prefer to borrow from friends and stay in less luxurious accommodations.

On the way back to the Praga, I noticed that my car was being tailed. Three men were close on my heels when I went inside, two took up positions by the reception desk, the third accompanied me upstairs to station himself outside our room. At dinner four men occupied a table close to ours, while another still guarded the entrance hall.

After dinner, I wrote a letter to Dr. Husák, giving a summary of the situation plus an intimation that if we were not allowed to cross the frontier on 28 November, I would start a hunger strike which I would maintain until our departure. Then I reported on the provocative and crude shadowing, adding: 'Presumably they want to provoke me to some unconsidered action, which, in view of their behaviour and their appearance, would not be so difficult.'

In conclusion, I wrote: 'I make no demands on you in this, my final letter, because I have come to the conclusion that to expect anything of you is futile. I merely wish to inform you about these matters and to remind you that he who encourages the use of despotic power and violence usually ends as the victim of the forces he has unleashed. Such is the inexorable logic of all revolutions, the French as much as the so-called socialist revolution. Once, already, you have had personal experience of this. I sincerely hope that you will not experience it again. You must surely be aware, however, that the gentlemen whose uncontrolled power is growing daily feel far greater hatred for you than for myself, because hatred always increases with the importance of its object. There are certain laws implicit in every civilized community and the consequences of infringing them are always tragic. In writing this I am concerned not with myself but rather with you and the power group you represent.'

The watchdogs were waiting outside as we left the hotel next morning to take the letter to Party headquarters. Seething with cold anger, I remarked at the top of my voice to Euženie as we passed them: 'Just take a good look at those dumb faces.' The one nearest took a step forward, then he retreated. He, too, felt an upsurge of anger, but his hands were tied—no doubt he wished they were free, as they had been when they had me in their clutches.

From Party headquarters we proceeded, with two cars in attendance, to feed Ucho. On turning into a side street near our home, I found the road blocked by a lorry, so, on the spur of the moment, I executed a U-turn and drove in my best rally style, finally taking refuge in a blind alley. We had shaken off our shadows and were free. Euženie walked home to feed Ucho while I drove into town. But soon I realized that not a soul in Prague was expecting me—we had said good-bye to everyone. Slowly I drove to the home of one of the 1968 politicians, but he was out. Then I searched for another friend, but he was neither at home nor at the garage where, being a doctor of philosophy, he is employed at a modest wage. Thoroughly depressed, I retired to another garage to have the car washed.

Our shadows were waiting at the hotel to resume their task. We decided to spend one more day in Prague, behaving peaceably in the hope they would withdraw, then we would be able to fetch our mother without betraying where she had been staying. And sure enough, in the morning the coast was clear. But Ucho spoilt everything by getting lost. By the time he turned up in the afternoon, the watchers were with us again.

As we drove out of Prague, we resolved to shake them off—partly to spare our friends, but mainly for the fun of it. However, two attempts at escape failed and by nightfall they were still following. Not far from our destination the main road takes a sharp right turn, while a secondary road leads straight ahead to the town of Sokolov. That gave me an idea—before reaching the turning, I extinguished my lights, then took the straight road, reckoning that when the lights disappeared they would think I had taken the bend. The ruse worked, and we were free. Soon after, we picked up my mother-in-law, who was in a terrible state of anxiety. Having reassured her, we had dinner at our hotel in almost festive mood, allowing ourselves wine when I had given my word that our money would last out for the few more days of waiting. I had written to the customs officers at the border that we would present ourselves at 7.00 a.m. on 28 November at the Pomezí frontier post.

During those last days we had many telephone calls from journalists, most frequently, of course, from Dick Verkijk. He told me that he had been at the frontier on the day of our abortive attempt, and a Czech lorry driver, who had overheard our conversation with the passport officer, had described what had happened. Whereupon Dick—the deported 'spy'—had calmly driven up to the frontier post to ask about Pachman. Having demanded his passport and kept him waiting about ten minutes, the guards said they knew nothing about anyone called Pachman, and ordered him to leave Czechoslovak territory immediately. Dick told me on the phone that this time he would keep away. They might have stopped me on his account—after all, we could engage in espionage the moment we met. But I knew, of course, that he was only saying this for the benefit of the authorities.

On Tuesday morning, 28 November, we arrived punctually to the minute. They kept us waiting one hour—a trifle compared with the first occasion—then they informed us that we must return to our hotel and await further instructions.

At the first barrier guarding the frontier crossing, Reuter's Prague correspondent was sitting in his car, observing the scene. I had exchanged a few words with him on the way to the post; now, on the return journey, I stopped and got out of the car, intending to have a longer talk. Since we were well outside the customs area, what we did was nobody else's business. However, a frontier guard came loping over in our direction, waving his automatic and yelling that we must drive away at once. When I objected that I saw no reason why we should leave, he aimed his weapon at me, shouting: 'Get moving, or I'll shoot!'

The Englishman made some comment, whereupon the guard aimed at him, then again at me. Telling the idiot that he had better be careful—supposing he fired by mistake—I suggested to the Reuter man that we drive to the hotel, but he decided to cross the frontier and soon he was telling his colleagues on the other side what had happened.

In the afternoon we had visitors. Four gentlemen announced that they came from police headquarters in Pilsen. 'We have to inform you,' they said, 'that you will be crossing the frontier today, but not at the Pomezí crossing. You will come with us; we will escort you and arrange for your departure.'

That meant, of course, that they wanted to keep us away from

the journalists. I assumed they would take us to the crossing at
Rozvadov. On leaving the hotel, I whispered to one of the staff,
'They're taking us via Rozvadov. If anyone inquires, tell them
that.' In Czechoslovakia today one can still trust people in the
less lucrative professions, including members of the ruling
working class—perhaps he would pass on the message!

Having taken the road to the south, our escort led us past the
turning to Rozvadov and continued along the frontier line. The
next possible crossing was at a place called Folmanov, but when
we stopped to tank up, they told us that we were heading for a
new frontier post, which they had to show me on the map—its
German name was Eisenerz. Soon we left the main road for
what was no more than a field track, then we were back on the
road, only to be taken along another obscure bye-way. Either the
driver was an idiot or they were pulling our legs, or . . . I hastily
dismissed the blackest thoughts. Probably they were determined
to make us really angry at this last moment.

Finally, I stopped, waved them over to our car, and insisted
that if we were not at the frontier by 6.30, I would return to
Prague. They promised that we would be there. By 6.30, however, we were in the Czech town of Klatovy, where I repeated my
threat. In surprisingly conciliatory tones they assured me that
we would drive by the quickest route and they even apologized
for the detours. At the frontier we would be through the formalities in ten minutes, they declared. So, again, I agreed to carry on.

This time we arrived at the frontier post, but we were not
finished in ten minutes. We had to carry all the locked luggage
and our bags containing things for the journey into the customs
house, where as usual the officers concentrated on documents and
pieces of paper. The inspection lasted two hours. Then we
carried everything back to the cars, while they photographed us
like mad—at least fifteen shots with flashes, perhaps for *Rudé
právo*? I wondered whether to assume a gay or a sad expression,
but then I decided it was best simply to wear the expressions we
happened to have.

All was ready, the engine running, our escort assembled with
the two customs officers. I thanked the latter, for they had helped

us carry the luggage and altogether they had behaved decently. They all stood in a row, and we in a row facing them. Then the head of the escort delivered a speech, the main purport of which was that we should be careful how we conducted ourselves abroad. If I confined myself to playing chess and refrained from engaging in politics, I could expect, in due course, to return home. I would play chess and everything would be as it used to be—but, 'If you engage in activity against the Republic, we shall find means even abroad to deal with you.'

So—after driving us like cattle along the frontier and landing us in a place I had never heard of, they had the impudence to lecture us. I retorted by thanking them for sending us, by night, to Munich of all places, where I had not planned to go, although I had friends in Radio Free Europe. Further, I requested them not to worry about my conduct. I was well aware how I should behave abroad, and I should be guided by that. Then, having bidden a warm farewell to the customs men, we drove off. Comenius wept on crossing the frontier; I felt no such desire—times have changed.

Our arrival at the Bavarian customs post caused some surprise. They knew all about us, but they had heard on the radio that we had been turned back, so how had we managed to get there? Instead of customs formalities, we had a friendly talk and I telephoned the DPA office in Munich asking them to book us rooms and let the waiting journalists know that we were safely over the border.

We drove down the hills until we joined the familiar Munich road. It was midnight, and by the time we had located the DPA office it was half-past one in the morning. As we entered the big office, Dick rushed forward to greet us—he had covered the distance from Schirnding where he had held his vigil in less time than it had taken us to drive from Eisenerz. Behind him stood Luboš Kaválek and his father. We hugged each other and talked, then my old friend, grandmaster Wolfgang Unzicker appeared with his wife, and several journalists, so that we held an impromptu press conference before retiring at last to bed.

Next day more journalists arrived. I did an interview with

young Kaválek for the Voice of America, and another with his father for Radio Free Europe, and more still for other journalists. And all the time we talked—in the end, I decided that the whole thing would have been quieter if they had let us cross as originally planned, there would have been less incitement under Article 100, less damaging of the interests of the Republic under Article 112, and less defaming under Articles 102, 103 and 104.

By the third morning my brain was pretty well addled, so we made our escape, arranging to meet Dick and the Dutch television people at the home of another chess friend, Lothar Schmid. And after lunch, we set off for Herr Evertz's house in Solingen.

On the autobahn we were swallowed up in the unending stream of cars, large and small. Our mother slept, twilight fell, lights conjured up strange images, notices and signs with the names of towns and motorway junctions swam past, and on and on. Ucho was sitting by the rear window, looking out at this strange new world. I knew this world, I had driven this route before, but alone, without my family. Everything in life returns, in the end— not in a closed circle, but by the spiral course described by the dialectics I used to study in my materialist days.

Circle, spiral—today I cannot be sure. I have lived through two revolutions and, perhaps, I have glimpsed some moments of a third. The first we fought under the banner of freedom and humanity against dire oppression and horrifying violence. The outcome brought new oppression and again violence. SS men were soaked in petrol and burned to death; Gestapo men were tortured under interrogation, and when the Protector of Bohemia and Moravia, K. H. Frank, moved to give the Nazi salute beneath the gallows, the executioner hit him and the crowd rejoiced. Then came the transfer of Germans from Czechoslovakia, and when I remarked at a meeting that this step was not in accord with the Marxist policy on nationalities as taught by J. V. Stalin, I was told: 'Comrade, it's a matter of shifting the frontiers of the Slav world westwards.' Within two years, the quarrel with Tito had made the Slavonic idea unfashionable— but, who knows, it may experience a revival.

During the second revolution, although confined to hospital, in spirit I was with the crowds of February 1948, singing 'away with tyrants and traitors all'. The road to socialism was open. Yet within six months the machine was at work again, devouring first the opponents, then the faithful upholders of the revolution. Revolutions always start with singing, and they end by devouring their own children. De Sade was right, not Marat.

I want no more part in revolution—let them devour whom they will next time. Yet I have an unhappy feeling that, despite all, I may, in my declining years, find myself mixed up with some foolish barricades again.

You must see that it's all pointless, my interrogator used to tell me. And there my friends sit in prison while the world, for the most part, turns a blind eye. Maybe it is pointless.

And yet it seems to me that everything in history makes sense— the trouble is simply that people are not wise enough to grasp what does and does not make sense. Close on two thousand years ago a man died. He was six hours dying, and he must have suffered greatly. He was not a pleasant sight, for the warders had beaten him. If any death was senseless, it must have been that death, for who would ever hear of it?

That death, however, made sense, certainly much more than anything else has ever done, only its meaning was not revealed at once or to everyone. True, one can say that this was no ordinary man, and that a death like his can happen only once. Yet nearly twenty centuries later, a man died—this time a very ordinary and very young man. He cried out with the pain of it, and he, too, died for others.

The modern gaolers even stole the headstone from his grave, that none should know where he lies. But every day fresh flowers mark the place, and flowers have at all times borne the same message, the message of hope and love.